I have decided

The Samuel Company Discipleship Handbook

MIKE HARPER

Copyright © 2018 Mike Harper

All rights reserved.

ISBN: 1976595355
ISBN-13: 978-1976595356

No part of this book may be reproduced, stored in a retrieval system, or transmitted by any means without the written permission of the Author.

"Scripture quotations marked (AMP) are taken from the Amplified® Bible, Copyright © 1954, 1958, 1962, 1964, 1965, 1987 by The Lockman Foundation Used by permission."
(www.Lockman.org)

"Scripture quotations marked (KJV) are taken from the King James Bible (KJV), *The Holy Bible, King James Version*. Cambridge Edition: 1769; *King James Bible Online*, 2017.
www.kingjamesbibleonline.org

"Scripture quotations marked (ESV) are from The ESV® Bible (The Holy Bible, English Standard Version®), copyright © 2001 by Crossway, a publishing ministry of Good News Publishers. Used by permission. All rights reserved."

This discipleship course was originally developed and taught at Ministry of Jesus Church in Dublin. We would like to thank all those who attended the initial training course, and especially Pastor Jayaseelan for allowing us that opportunity.

CONTENTS

	Introduction	Pg #i
1	Sin & Law	Pg #1
2	Salvation & Repentance	Pg #14
3	Grace & Sanctification	Pg #23
4	Hearing from God	Pg #34
5	Intimate Prayer	Pg #45
6	Intimate Worship	Pg #55
7	Power of Words	Pg #66
8	Humility	Pg #76
9	Faith	Pg #85
10	The life of a disciple	Pg #92
11	The call of God	Pg #100
12	The cost	Pg #109
	Challenge answers	Pg #114

I have decided

This book is designed to be used over a period of twelve-weeks to help people develop in their walk with God. There will be many topics and concepts covered in the Sections to follow, but the most important thing is that you have decided that 'I want to follow Jesus and to be His disciple'. You might be a new believer, or perhaps have attended church for years but have never taken your walk seriously. No matter the beginning, I hope that by the end of this course you will be in a better position to stand firmly and declare the Light of Jesus in an ever-darkening world.

To begin, I want to introduce you to some of what the Scriptures reveal about the nature of God. As people experienced God, they often named Him according to those attributes. "Elohim" is the first name for God found in the Bible, and it's used over two-thousand three-hundred times throughout the Old Testament. Elohim comes from the Hebrew root meaning "strength" or "power" and has the unusual characteristic of being plural in form. While the plural meaning may have been a mystery for many centuries, this later became understood as pointing towards the Trinity; God the Father, Jesus and the Holy Spirit. Elohim is our Creator.

> *"In the beginning God [Elohim] created the heavens and the earth"* **Genesis 1:1** KJV

"El" is another name people used for God in the Bible, showing up about two-hundred times in the Old Testament. *El* is the simple form arising from *Elohim* and is often combined with other words to describe attributes of God. For Example, El Shaddai, which means 'Almighty God' is used in this verse:

> *"Even by the God of thy father, who shall help thee; and by the Almighty, who shall bless thee with blessings of heaven above, blessings of the deep that lieth under, blessings of the breasts, and of the womb"* **Genesis 49:25** KJV

Biblical history reveals that sin entered the world through Adam and Eve. God always knew that Adam and Eve would sin, and therefore He always had a solution prepared for us. Scripture tells us that *"The eyes of the Lord are everywhere"* **Proverbs 15:3**. We must understand that God is outside of time. So God already knows how we will live our lives because He can see it all in advance. Yes, we still have free will. It's just that God knows where that free will is going to take us. The solution came to us initially as a promise to Abram:

Now the LORD had said unto Abram, Get thee out of thy country, and from thy kindred, and from thy father's house, unto a land that I will shew thee; And I will make of thee a great nation, and I will bless thee, and make thy name great; and thou shalt be a blessing: And I will bless them that bless thee, and curse him that curseth thee: and in thee shall all families of the earth be blessed" **Genesis 12:1-3 KJV**

Any promise from God is valuable because He is faithful and every Word He speaks will be fulfilled. There is a reason why King David called God his Rock [**Psalm 144:1**]. The Scriptures say of Him, *"He is the Rock, his work is perfect: for all his ways are judgment: a God of truth and without iniquity, just and right is he."* **Deuteronomy 32:4** KJV. In fact, even if we do not remain faithful, He will remain faithful to us because He *"cannot deny Himself"* **2 Timothy 2:13**. Any word that goes out from the mouth of God will not return void [**Isaiah 55:11**]. Therefore, if God makes a promise, then it will be fulfilled.

Abram obeyed God and left his country and people. Despite the promises he received, Abram saw that his wife was barren and asked God, *"what can you give me since I remain childless"* **Genesis 15:1**. Abram also then asked about the promised land, saying *"how can I know that I will gain possession of it?"* **Genesis 15:8**. So God listened to Abram's plea for a sign and granted him a legal agreement called a covenant. In that process, both Abram and his wife gained a new identity. Abram became Abraham and Sarai became Sarah [**Genesis 17**]. This agreement was for Abraham and all his descendants. The blood-ratified covenant had four specific elements which included (a) a proposal (b) an acceptance of the proposal (c) a blood sacrifice and (d) a meal.

Four-hundred years later when Abraham's descendants departed from Egypt, Moses led them to the mountain of the Lord. Here the Lord God wished to reaffirm with them a covenant of promise. However, while Moses was receiving God's commandments, the Israelites fell into the sin of idolatry. They broke the covenant and to do so carried a death penalty. God was about to destroy them and instead make a new nation with just Moses [**Exodus 32:10**], but Moses interceded for his people. So, then God imposed on Israel the Book of the Law, based around the high priesthood of Aaron, and it became their task-master until Jesus came to pay the penalty. Not only would the death penalty be paid but there would also be a New Covenant.

The prophets Ezekiel and Jeremiah both prophesied that God would make a New Covenant, not like the broken one, but one that God would write on the hearts of people and that they shall *"know the Lord"* [**Ezekiel 11:19, 36:26, Jeremiah 31:31-34**]. The word 'Lord' which is translated from the Hebrew word 'YHWH' is central to this prophecy.

YHWH is found more often in the Old Testament than any other name for God, approximately seven thousand times. YHVH comes from the Hebrew verb "to be" and is the name that God disclosed to Moses at the burning bush. *God said to Moses, "I AM THAT I AM: and he said, Thus shalt thou say unto the children of Israel, I AM hath sent me unto you. And God said moreover unto Moses, Thus shalt thou say unto the children of Israel, The LORD God of your fathers, the God of Abraham, the God of Isaac, and the God of Jacob, hath sent me unto you: this is my name for ever, and this is my memorial unto all generations"* **Exodus 3:14-15** KJV

The LORD who revealed Himself as YHVH in the Old Testament is revealed as Jesus in the New Testament. Jesus shares the same attributes as YHVH and declares to be YHVH. In the gospel of John, Jesus presents himself as the "I AM." When confronted by some Jewish leaders regarding His claim of seeing Abraham (who lived some 2000 years earlier), Jesus replied, *"Truly, truly, I say to you, before Abraham was born, I am." Then took they up stones to cast at him: but Jesus hid himself, and went out of the temple, going through the midst of them, and so passed by"* **John 8:58-59** KJV. Those Jewish leaders understood that Jesus was claiming to be YHVH. So they tried to stone Him to death for what they considered blasphemy under Jewish Law.

In the Book of Romans, Paul declares, *"if you confess with your mouth that Jesus is Lord and believe in your heart that God raised him from the dead, you will be saved"* **Romans 10:9** ESV. Immediately after that, in Romans 10:13, Paul backs up this declaration by quoting from the Joel 2:32, *"For whosoever shall call upon the name of the Lord shall be saved"* **Romans 10:13** KJV. Calling on Yeshua (Jesus) as Lord is the same as calling Him YHVH because Yeshua (Jesus) is YHVH (LORD), the Messiah foretold throughout the entire Old Testament.

YHWH, just like El was often combined with other words to describe attributes. For example, YHWH Rophe, which means the Lord who heals, was used in the Old Testament (e.g. **Exodus 15:26**). This name is another example of how YHWH is revealed as Jesus. One messianic prophecy declared that the sun of righteousness would rise with healing in its wings [**Malachi 4:2**]. In fulfilment of this, many people were healed by Jesus as He walked the earth, but the most profound healing came on the cross because *"by his wounds we are healed"* [**Isaiah 53:5; 1 Peter 2:24**]. The four gospels bear testimony to these healings and His death and resurrection:

> *"And the people, when they knew it, followed him: and he received them, and spake unto them of the kingdom of God, and healed them that had need of healing"* **Luke 9:11** KJV

> *"And as they were afraid, and bowed down their faces to the earth, they said*

unto them, Why seek ye the living among the dead? He is not here, but is risen: remember how he spake unto you when he was yet in Galilee" **Luke 24:5-6** KJV

We also find Jesus using the words 'I AM' in His teachings:

"Jesus said to them, I AM the bread of life; whoever comes to me shall not hunger, and whoever believes in me shall never thirst" **John 6:35** ESV

"Then spake Jesus again unto them, saying, I AM the light of the world: he that followeth me shall not walk in darkness, but shall have the light of life" **John 8:12** KJV

"Jesus said to him, I AM the way, and the truth, and the life. No one comes to the Father except through me" **John 14:6** ESV

"I AM the true vine, and my Father is the husbandman" **John 15:1** KJV

"Jesus said unto her, I AM the resurrection, and the life: he that believeth in me, though he were dead, yet shall he live" **John 11:25** KJV

It is through the life, death and resurrection of Jesus that we come to know God as our Redeemer. We need a Redeemer because we broke the Law and the penalty is death. When Paul spoke of this, he said that Jesus *"who gave himself for us to redeem us from all lawlessness and to purify for himself a people for his own possession who are zealous for good works"* **Titus 2:14** ESV.

Up until Jesus sacrifice', the priests usually took a sacrificial lamb at the time of Passover and made a sacrifice. This sacrifice was always carried out by the high priest. However, Jesus entered Jerusalem as a perfect Lamb, ready for slaughter. Not only did He enter by the same gate that the sacrificial lambs came in by, but he would also die at the same time as the Passover sacrifice. When he appeared before the Levitical high priest, the meeting ended with the Levitical high priest tearing his own clothes. This act, according to the Law of Moses, removed his spiritual office as the high priest. Instead, the spiritual authority passed to Jesus. There could only be one official sacrifice that year, and so Jesus died as the High Priest and as the Lamb of God [Revelation 5:12]:

"But this man, because he continueth ever, hath an unchangeable priesthood. Wherefore he is able also to save them to the uttermost that come unto God by him, seeing he ever liveth to make intercession for them. For such an high priest became us, who is holy, harmless, undefiled, separate from sinners, and made higher than the heavens; Who needeth not daily, as those high priests, to offer up sacrifice, first for his own sins, and then for the people's: for this he did once,

when he offered up himself. For the law maketh men high priests which have infirmity; but the word of the oath, which was since the law, maketh the Son, who is consecrated for evermore" **Hebrews 7:24-28** KJV

This sacrifice was the establishment of the New Covenant that Ezekiel and Jeremiah had prophesied. We see the same four elements as the Old Covenant. There was a proposal, a promise, an acceptance and a meal. A pattern that Jesus will complete when He returns.

Now, when a person accepts Jesus, their spirit is made new, and so they live under the New Covenant. The departure from the Old Covenant means that they are no longer circumcised in the old manner, but their hearts are circumcised [**Deuteronomy 30:6**]. The laws are no longer written on stone, they are written on their hearts [**Hebrews 10:16**]. This change means that they are not slaves to the Law of Moses [**Galatians 4:21-31**], nor should they fall back into lawlessness [**Matthew 7:23**]. Instead, they must know YHWH, love Him and obey Him. Indeed, they should love God with all their hearts and love their neighbours [**Mark 12:30-31**]. They are to live by the Spirit of God, allowing their minds to be transformed [**Galatians 5:25, Ephesians 4:23**]. They are to leave behind their old life and the ways of the world, and follow Jesus their Messiah wherever He might lead them [**Romans 12:2, Proverbs 3:6**].

This is the good news! We can be set free from the slavery of sin, and start afresh with a brand-new heart.

However, God has not just called us just so that we can be set free from our sin and know Him more. He also has a job for us, namely to be one of His disciples. When Jesus called on His disciples to follow Him, He said to them "Come and I will make you fishers of men." Later, Jesus entrusted them with what became known as the 'great commission', which simply means to go out into the world and to make disciples. This task is what we, as His modern-day disciples must also do. Our purpose is even more amazing because each of us has our own calling and jobs to accomplish. One disciple may work the harvest fields to plough and to plant the seed. Another may come along and bring in a harvest of a thousand souls. No one is greater than the other. We are to listen and obey God.

I pray that we, as His disciples, will be faithful to achieve all that He has set out for us to accomplish until the great and mighty day of His return. May God find us busy in the fields and with plenty of oil in our lamps.

I also wish to introduce you to the Bible itself, which believers also call the 'Word of God'. The Bible consists of sixty-six different books which were written by about forty people in total. The Biblical texts were composed in three different languages which were Hebrew, Aramaic, and Greek. The writers came from almost every social rank including political leaders, peasants, kings, herdsmen, fishermen, priests, tax-gatherers, tentmakers, educated and uneducated, Jews and Gentiles. Most of the writers were unknown to each other, and writing at various periods over a range of about 1600 years[1]. In other words, the Bible is rooted and grounded in history. Despite this, as a whole, it deals with the matter of the redemption of mankind.

In the same way that people such as Abraham experienced God and named Him according to His attributes, God gave revelation to people to write the Bible. In the process of production, we should envisage God as the editor of the individual authors, inspiring and guiding them as to what to include or exclude. For example, let us consider when Abraham took Isaac up the mountain to make a sacrifice. The record explains that after the event that Abraham came down the mountain. It does not name Isaac although he probably accompanied his father. There was no mention of Isaac until he was united with his bride (Genesis 24:4). He is seemingly edited out of the text, but why? The answer is that editor, the Holy Spirit, wanted this event to point to Jesus. After Jesus sacrifice and ascension, He will not be seen again until He returns for His bride. This record of Abraham and Isaac, along with many more similar instances, point to a higher power guiding and instructing the authors. We should recognise that God inspired the authors to write their words so that we could read them and come to know Him. Therefore, we should accept the Bible as literal truth.

Bible Gateway explains that 'The Bible is the revelation of God to people. If we believe that there is a God who created us and endowed us with minds that are capable of acquiring and dispensing knowledge, of adjusting ourselves to God's creation and to a degree controlling and improving the conditions under which we live, then it is only reasonable to assume that God can communicate with us and disclose to us who He is, what He expects of us, and in turn what we can expect of Him.'[2]

There are two major sections in the Bible, namely the 'Old Testament' and the 'New Testament'. The Old Testament consists of thirty-nine Books, and it was written over many centuries. It includes all the books predating the birth of Jesus. Scholars observe that there were oral traditions as well as written accounts. The records were preserved on parchment, or animal skins, so the report of God's dealing with His people would never be forgotten. The parchments were rolled up into scrolls, and over the centuries

---

[1] https://www.biblegateway.com/resources/eastons-bible-dictionary/Bible

[2] https://www.biblegateway.com/resources/asbury-bible-commentary/General-Introduction

more manuscripts were written and added to the collection.

The New Testament consists of twenty-seven books, and it is believed to be written over a fifty-year period from about 45 to 95 AD. It is made up of books which record witness statements of Jesus' ministry and the beginning of His church after His death and resurrection. The New Testament or rather the "New Covenant" (Luke 22:20), is the Covenant of Grace - it succeeds to the old broken covenant (the Old Testament) of works.

Listed below are the four first books which are witness accounts of Jesus life and ministry:

Matthew — How Jesus is related to the Old Testament.

Mark — The shortest and quickest action-packed overview.

Luke — How Jesus related to the poor, the disadvantaged, and to women.

John — The personal, most intimate and reflective portrait of Jesus.

The earliest Christians did not have Bibles, but some believers did have access to the Torah, the Psalms, the books of the Major and Minor Prophets and so on (the contents of the Old Testament). However, as time went on it became more and more essential to have written and reliable accounts from the Apostles to share with new believers. For example, the writings of Paul the Apostle included letters addressed to specific churches, which would have been copied and shared with other believers. The Jews had a heritage of making accurate copies of the Torah, which was perhaps something passed on to the early church.

For many centuries the Bible had to be copied by hand, word for word, but times have changed. Since the innovation of the Gutenberg press in the 1450's, the Bible has become the most circulated book in the world. More copies have been published and distributed than any other book. In the last year, publishers produced over sixty-million complete Bibles, ninety-million New Testaments and over 1.5 billion scripture sections in over two-thousand languages[3].

---

[3] www.visionvideo.com/files/DTB_ColorBookLR.pdf

What the Bible Says About Itself:

It is profiting - "All scripture is given by inspiration of God, and is profitable for doctrine, for reproof, for correction, for instruction in righteousness" **2 Timothy 3:16** KJV.

Illuminating - "Thy word is a lamp unto my feet, and a light unto my path" **Psalm 119:105** KJV.

It penetrates - "For the word of God is quick, and powerful, and sharper than any two-edged sword, piercing even to the dividing asunder of soul and spirit, and of the joints and marrow, and is a discerner of the thoughts and intents of the heart" **Hebrews 4:12** KJV.

Guiding - "How can a young man keep his way pure? By guarding it according to your word... I have stored up your word in my heart, that I might not sin against you" **Psalms 119:9,11** ESV.

Enduring - "Do not think that I have come to abolish the Law or the Prophets; I have not come to abolish them but to fulfil them. 18 For truly, I say to you, until heaven and earth pass away, not an iota, not a dot, will pass from the Law until all is accomplished" **Matthew 5:17-18** ESV.

God-Speaking - "Long ago, at many times and in many ways, God spoke to our fathers by the prophets, but in these last days he has spoken to us by his Son, whom he appointed the heir of all things, through whom also he created the world" **Hebrews 1:1-2** ESV.

Practical Guide
How do I use this course?
Design

This course is divided into twelve Sections, each of which should take you a week to complete. These twelve Sections are then divided up into four Blocks, listed below:

Block 1: The Basics

    Week One   Sin & Law

    Week Two   Salvation & repentance

    Week Three   Grace & Sanctification

Block 2: Relationship with God

    Week Four   Hearing from God

    Week Five   Intimate prayer

    Week Six   Intimate worship

Block 3: Daily living

    Week Seven   The power of words

    Week Eight   Humility

    Week Nine   Faith

Block 4: The Mission

    Week Ten   The Life of a Disciple

    Week Eleven   The Call of God

    Week Twelve   The Cost

Assignments

Each Section has challenges for you to complete, these will alternate between practical and written assignments. It is vital that you try to complete these tasks to the best of your ability. The practical assignments will give you some fundamental experience in talking with people and sharing the good news. The written assessments, on the other hand, are aimed at evaluating where you currently stand with God and encouraging you to grow closer to God. Many of these written assessments may contain information that you might wish to keep private. You do not need to share the information with anyone.

Video training

In each Section, you may find references to our YouTube channel where you can watch complimentary videos to accompany this course. If you go to our YouTube channel 'Revival Well' and then go to our Playlists, you will find one called 'Discipleship Course'. In that Playlist, you will see all the videos relating this course. You can also view or download all the videos directly from Google Drive at this link:

https://drive.google.com/open?id=1hUtub8yUfxczn6awBeqm3qSu7w4zICIA

Gifts assessment & Certificate

If you would like to do a spiritual gifts assessment after you complete your course, we can send you out the form by email. If you would like a certificate for completing the course, email us with the following information: First Name, Surname, Nationality, Date of Birth and address.

    Contact email: info@revivalwell.org

I HAVE DECIDED

MIKE HARPER

Testimonies about this course:

"Each lesson was well organized, straight to the point and not too heavy i.e. there was not a sense of overwhelment. The video jams that accompanied the lessons were impactful. The homework was a very necessary challenge which got me out of my comfort zone and into a zone I believe God wants for me. This discipleship course came at a time in my life where I needed to be encouraged to go out there and answer God's call to reach out to the lost. Each topic lead me to a deeper search of God's truth and will in my life but also a self-examination. I was challenged on how and why I do things in my daily walk with Christ. Ultimately, I am left with a desire to boldly serve God in Spirt and in Truth, to do away with religiousity and become a remnant to the Glory of God. We appreciate you and pray for more people to be blessed by this."

Disciple, Dublin

"This course has truly been a blessing to me and my family. The material was clear and concise with an element of a challenge, which is necessary. May God bless you for all the hard work put into this. The seeds have been sown on this occasion. By God's grace these seeds will bear fruits, good fruits. Amen. My testimony can be described with the Bible verse found in Romans 12:2. This discipleship course has indeed 'transformed' the way I perceive God's will and the importance of seeking His Kingdom above all things. Although we are to give to Caesar what belongs to Caesar, we need to give God what belongs to Him. This course has helped me reconnect with the areas which our Father is requiring of me."

Disciple, Dublin

Sin & Law
Section One

Introduction

Welcome to the first Block of your discipleship course. This first Block is made up of three Sections which you should aim to complete over a period of three weeks. The course begins with this week's lesson about 'Sin and Law'. Whether you have heard this foundational teaching before or you are hearing about it for the very first time, after you finish this Section of this course, we want you to (a) have a good understanding of God's Law and (b) be equipped to teach others.

Now please access our video media and watch **discipleship training, Video 1**

If you go to our YouTube channel 'Revival Well' and then go to our Playlists, you will find one called 'Discipleship Course'. In that Playlist, you will see all the videos relating this course. Click on the one called 'Video1. I have decided. Introduction'. Alternatively, you can view or download the video directly from Google Drive at this link:

https://drive.google.com/open?id=1hUtub8yUfxczn6awBeqm3qSu7w4zICIA

Civil Law versus God's Law

As citizens of a nation, we should be at least familiar with our laws. This type of law, namely Civil Law, can be defined as 'the system of rules which a particular community or country recognises as regulating the actions of its members and which it may enforce by the imposition of penalties'[4]. From this definition, we see that law has three primary elements to understand:

1. The rules (for example it is illegal to drink and drive)
2. The people it applies to (the people of a nation)
3. The penalties for not obeying the rules (for example, a fine or a prison sentence)

In theory, this system of laws and penalties should work fine but, that is not always the case. Quite often people in our society break the rules but don't get caught, most likely because the enforcement was not adequate. Then at other times, people may have been caught breaking the law but then they are set free later. This lapse can happen for various reasons such as a lack of evidence. The penalty then is not a fixed matter. Penalties can vary between nations and within nations. Some judges may show leniency. Others may not. Furthermore, once the sentence is received, it can be reduced later (for good behaviour) or may indeed be quashed after an appeal. Finally, some people are wrongfully convicted of crimes that they did not commit.

So, we see that Civil Law, while upholding our societies, is flawed because its application is not always fair or just. Justice bears down heavily on some, while not at all on others.

Here lies the distinction between Civil Law and God's Laws:

1. Gods' Law is *holy*: because it is holy, it cannot approve of sin in any form, and so it condemns any sinner. God's enforcement rate is 100%, everyone who breaks the Law has a penalty waiting for them.
2. God's Law is *just*: because it is just, it cannot show mercy to those who have broken the Law. The penalty for not obeying the law is 100% just because God knows everything. He saw all the actions, thoughts and words and judges us righteously by them. The punishment is the same for everyone who breaks His laws. There is no leniency or special cases **Romans 6:23**.
3. God's Law is *perfect*: because it is perfect, there are no errors or loopholes. God's Law applies to everyone. You can't escape it **Hebrews 4:13**. Leaving the

---

[4] Online definition https://www.google.ie/?gws_rd=ssl#q=definition+of+law accessed June 2016

country won't help. Hiding in a cave won't help. Even becoming an astronaut won't help.

God's strict level of justice is linked directly to His holiness. His laws reveal the nature of His holiness and holy standards. The Bible gives us God's commands but also shows us that no one can keep them. Thus, without God's intervention, all of humanity is subject to the penalty for falling short of God's standards **Romans 3:23**. So, we see that God's Law is very different to human laws. However, it does still have the same three elements: rules, people it applies to and penalties. We will now take each of these in turn.

The Rules

In living the Christian life, do you think God's Law is important to you? Give three reasons why:

_____
_____
_____

There are many reasons why God's Law should be important to Christians. For example (a) to evangelise (b) to know what we are saved from (c) to know how to obey (d) to know how to overcome the enemy and (e) to understand sin.

To get an example from Scripture, read the following verses in your Bible:

1 Samuel 7:3-11

In your own words, state what Samuel did which illustrates the importance of obeying God's Law:

_____
_____
_____

Samuel was a prophet who heard the voice of God, but he also knew the laws given by God to Moses. What Law did Samuel enact, that helped his people win the battle against the Philistines?

*Before you write your answer, read **Deuteronomy 28:1&7** and consider the application of these verses in the life of Samuel.*

_____
_____

This specific law from Deuteronomy states that *'if you will fully obey the Lord Your God'* then *'The Lord will grant that the enemies who rise up against you will be defeated'*. Samuel knew that the nation of Israel had been in disobedience but he also knew the solution. So, he called on Israel to fast and repent and after they followed his instructions, their enemy was defeated.

If Samuel could use this law to help him when he was under attack, then we should also consider using it in our own lives. There are always battles to be fought and won. When an attack comes, we should seek the Lord and ask Him to reveal any sin in our lives. Then we should turn and repent of it, and trust in God to win the battle for us. We could apply the same law to churches and even nations. Take a moment to think about the history of your nation. Is there any history of invasion by another nation? Perhaps the people were in rebellion against God. These are profound matters that we can consider and discuss with God.

Indeed, this one specific example of law is just a small sample of the knowledge that we can gain from knowing God's Laws and how to apply them to our lives. We should also consider what would have happened in Samuel's day if Israel had not repented.

Write out this verse: **Deuteronomy 28:25**

_____

_____

This verse reveals what the scripture declares: *"my people are destroyed for lack of wisdom"* **Hosea 4:6**. Take a few moments in prayer and ask God to reveal the Word of God so that you may come to understand it and how to apply it to your life.

The people the Law applies to

There are different laws that God has given. There are natural laws such as gravity – such laws are constant. There are also spiritual laws which are constant too. In the introduction to this course, we touched upon the background to this and the promises which were given to Abraham. But let's go back to the very beginning and look at what happened at creation.

Read the following verses in your Bible: **Genesis 1: 1-31**

When God created the world, was there such a thing as sin? *Examine verse 31.*

_____

In this verse, we see that after the fifth day of creation, that all things were *'very good'*. This statement means that it must have been at some point after this that sin entered the world. Most people know the story, even if they aren't Christians. When God created Adam and Eve, He gave them one law or rule. There wasn't much that they had to obey in comparison to the laws that Moses received. Even still, Adam and Eve stumbled with the simple rule.

Read the following verses in your Bible to remind yourself of the story: **Genesis 3:2-7**

From this one act of disobedience by Adam and Eve, sin spread to all humanity:

> *"Wherefore, as by one man sin entered into the world, and death by sin; and so death passed upon all men, for that all have sinned"* **Romans 5:12** KJV

What this means for us is that we are born with an inheritance of a sinful nature **Romans 3:23** that originates from Adam and Eve. This fallen nature is an iniquity **Psalm 51:1-6** that causes a bias in our hearts, meaning that it convinces us that evil things are good, and good things are evil. Then each time we sin, we are acting in rebellion against God. These are our transgressions against God's Laws **Psalm 32:1-5**.

For now, I want you to think of sin like this:

Sin = disobeying God

This is unavoidable for us and mere forgiveness is not enough, we need a whole new nature **2 Corinthians 5:17**.

Knowledge Challenge #1 [Answer on page 114]

Arrange these numbers in the correct numerical sequence:

34   5   3   2   21   0   1   8   1   13

_____

This sequence of numbers are the first numbers in what has become known as the Fibonacci sequence. It was named after the Italian mathematician who introduced the pattern to Western European mathematics in 1202. However, other mathematicians across the world had also stumbled across this very same sequence as far back as the year 200.

Why is this sequence of any importance at all to our understanding of Law?

In the same way that you find signatures on artwork, this mathematical sequence has been dubbed as 'God's fingerprint'. You will see that many things in nature appear according to this sequence. For example, the spiral shapes of waves in the ocean, the spiral shape of plants such as the pine cone or pineapple, the spiral of our fingerprints, the size of bones in human hands, and many more examples. It is direct scientific evidence of the Creator.

Now please access our video media and watch **discipleship training, Video 2**

If you go to our YouTube channel 'Revival Well' and then go to our Playlists, you will find one called 'Discipleship Course'. In that Playlist, you will see all the videos relating this course. Click on the one called 'Video2. I have decided. God's Fingerprint'. Alternatively, you can view or download the video directly from Google Drive at this link:

https://drive.google.com/open?id=1hUtub8yUfxczn6awBeqm3qSu7w4zICIA

God didn't just leave a fingerprint in mathematics. He wrote His Law into the fabric of our Universe! To understand this concept of God's Laws existing in such a way, let's take an example from the laws given to Moses:

> "Whoever takes a human life shall surely be put to death" **Leviticus 24:17** ESV

How can such a law be written into the fabric of the Universe? Well, if I am correct, then you would assume that there would be a scientist or mathematician who would have also discovered this same rule mentioned above. Well, there is! It is called Newton's Third Law, which states:

> For every action, there is an equal and opposite reaction[5]

Of course, Newton made his observations concerning small objects. But the same Law applies no matter how big the objects are, or how complicated the interaction is. The

---

[5] Online definition https://www.google.ie/?gws_rd=ssl#q=newtons+third+law accessed June 2016

wider public also notes this Law, except they explain it this way – *'What goes around comes around'*. Certainly, this goes some way to describe what was written in **Romans 1:20**, that God is evident in nature.

The most important thing we should take note of is that a person cannot avoid God's Law. Every single person is subject to these laws because they exist in the Universe. You can't escape them or hide from them. This topic is something to share about when talking with unbelievers, explaining to them how God's law matches scientific laws and common-sense laws, leading on to the salvation message.

The penalties for breaking the Law

Generations after Adam, Moses was given the Law to teach the people of Israel. Many people think that the Law did not exist until that moment. However, we should consider that the Law has probably always existed because (a) the Word of God, Jesus, has always existed **John 1,** and (b) there are records of transgressions against God before Moses. For example, the commandment *'Thou shall not kill'* was given to Moses, but this law was also discovered by Cain when he killed his brother Abel and received judgement because of what he had done **Genesis 4:11-12**. Another example is when God judged the whole world for their corruption and sent a flood to destroy them **Genesis 6:12**. Only Noah and his family were saved. Wherever there are the Words of God, there are commands, and the commands *are* Law. We will look at this in more detail as we continue.

Open your Bible and write out these verses:

Romans 3:23

_____

_____

_____

Romans 4:15a

_____

_____

_____

From these verses, we see that everyone is subject to the Law, that all of us fall short of the Law – meaning that we constantly break the Law. The result of this law-breaking will result in wrath. Therefore:

If sin = disobeying God

Then...

The Law = Rules to avoid the penalty

It makes perfect sense to say this because the Law shows us ways to avoid God's wrath. It is imperative for us to understand and to know the Law. Knowing it is one thing, but keeping it is impossible.

When most of us think of the Law of Moses, we think of the 'Ten commandments' in **Exodus 20:12-17**. However, the Law of Moses is much more complicated than ten simple rules. The books of Exodus, Leviticus and Numbers outline around 613 commandments in total. Now, you've probably not even heard these commands, let alone tried to obey them. Here is an interesting question to consider at this point, are God's Laws restricted to these 613 commands? Write your thoughts below:

_____
_____
_____

An example you could use to think about this is the book of Jonah. Most of us know the story, of how Jonah set out to avoid what God wanted him to do, and when he finally obeyed and brought a message of impending judgement to Nineveh, they repented and the destruction was avoided **Jonah 3:6-10**. It can be challenging for many Christians to understand the will of God. If Jonah prophesied destruction, but it didn't happen, does that make him a false prophet? If God said that Nineveh would be destroyed then why was it not destroyed?

Although God relented at the time, many years later the city was destroyed. So God's judgment was still delivered, however, so was His mercy through Jonah. There are certain things that we can be sure of, and one is that God's words do not return void **Isaiah 55:11**. It was true of the destruction of Nineveh, even though Jonah had his doubts at the time. The second thing that we are sure of is that Jesus is the Word of God, and He never stops speaking. The Bible is a written record of the Word of God, but the Word of God (Jesus) is not restricted to the Bible. The Word of God instead, is living and active **John 1:14**.

For example, imagine today is a Wednesday and Jesus instructs you, 'Go down to your local supermarket, there you will see a lady in a plaster-cast, I want you to pray for her.' Now that command certainly does not exist in the 613 commandments of Exodus, Leviticus and Numbers. Nor is a supermarket mentioned in the New Testament. However, it remains a command, and if I were to hear it and disobey, then I would be acting in sin. Every single day, Jesus has things that He has planned for us to complete **Ephesians 2:10**. So every day we risk falling into sin unless we are hearing God's step by step guidance, recognising it and then obeying it.

Have you ever asked God in prayer, "What would You like me to do today?" Have you ever felt something on your heart from God urging you to go and do something?

_____

If so, what happened? Did you obey? If you ignored it, did you feel convicted afterwards? Write your answer here:

_____
_____
_____

When the law was first given to Moses, it was a written Law **Exodus 34**. They were clearly set out rules which the people could follow. Why then, was attempting to comply to that Law always going to end up in failure? Write your thoughts on this:

_____
_____
_____

Imagine that you have a job working in an office. Now there are some office rules. One such rule is that you cannot use the company printer and paper for your own personal printing needs. Having taken a pay-cut in the previous year, you decide to use the printer on Saturdays while no-one is around. Have you ever done something like this? The truth is that written rules are very easy to break!

Now imagine a slightly changed perspective. You still work in the office, and they have the same rule about not using the company printer. However, this time it is a family run business, owned by your brother. Last night your sister-in-law came to visit your house and cried on your shoulder because of the financial stress that your brother is facing. Every day you see him arriving to work, hurting because the company has hit a rough patch. He has been depressed for several months, and everyone in the family is worried about him. Now, would you still go and use that printer on a Saturday morning while you are alone? It's much harder isn't it when it tugs at your heart.

Therefore, it was good news that Jeremiah prophesied concerning a New Covenant:

> *But this shall be the covenant that I will make with the house of Israel; After those days, saith the LORD, I will put my law in their inward parts, and write it in their hearts; and will be their God, and they shall be my people. And they shall teach no more every man his neighbour, and every man his brother, saying, Know the LORD: for they shall all know me, from the least of them unto the greatest of them, saith the LORD: for I will forgive their iniquity, and I will remember their sin no more"* **Jeremiah 31:33-34** KJV

What this means is that followers of Jesus are set free from the Law of Moses: the written Law does not apply to us anymore. If we could have obeyed the Law of Moses, it would have saved us, but no one could keep the Law. So instead of saving us, the Law acted to condemn us **Romans 8:3**. Thank God that He replaced it with the New Covenant and *"all that matters is faith which is expressed through love"* **Galatians 5:6**. How do we then express this love to God? Jesus spoke about this saying:

> *"Jesus answered him, If anyone loves me, he will keep my word, and my Father will love him, and we will come to him and make our home with him. Whoever does not love me does not keep my words. And the word that you hear is not mine but the Father's who sent me"* **John 14:23-24** ESV

Some might use grace to declare that they are free to sin because they are not under the Law anymore. However, in the Book of Galatians, Paul defines two types of people: those who live by the Spirit and those who live by the flesh **Galatians 5:16-24**. It is only those who are living by the Spirit that are not under the Law. A person living by the flesh is given over to sinful desires, eagerly wishing to declare their freedom to commit sins. Those who live in such a way will not inherit the kingdom of God. Therefore, we are not given freedom to sin. Instead, we are given *freedom from sin*.

Now, **take five minutes** to think of any situation or sin that may have come up as a part of this Section, repent to God and ask His forgiveness.

SECTION ONE CHALLENGE

In the following section, you are going to be asked some very personal questions. The answers to these questions should be 100% private between you and God. If necessary, please answer using a separate piece of paper and discard it after use.

What is the worst sin you have ever committed? Describe when it happened and how you reconciled with God.

_____
_____
_____
_____

What is the least sin that you have ever committed? Describe when it happened and how you reconciled with God.

_____
_____
_____
_____

Without looking up your Bible, list out the Ten Commandments:

1. _____
2. _____
3. _____
4. _____
5. _____
6. _____
7. _____
8. _____
9. _____
10. _____

Now check in your Bible, how many did you get right? **Exodus 20:1-17**

_____

How many of these commandments do you think you might have broken?

_____
_____
_____
_____

Look up these verses and write them out below: **Matthew 5:21-22**

_____
_____
_____
_____
_____
_____
_____
_____

After reading this, do you think you have broken more commandments than you originally thought?

_____
_____
_____
_____

Can you identify any patterns of sin in your life? (Pattern meaning something which keeps coming up over and over which used to be/still is a struggle). For example, a tendency to lie to a sibling. List these patterns here:

_____
_____
_____
_____
_____
_____
_____

Is it right to think that these things are just 'part of who we are'?

Write out this verse: **2 Corinthians 5:17**

_____
_____
_____
_____

If the old has gone, but we are still sinning, why is that happening?

Write out this verse **Romans 12:2**

_____
_____
_____
_____

What is the worst thing that you have ever done to a person whom you loved? How did you resolve what you did? Did you go to them and apologise and ask for forgiveness? Did you have to swear that you would never do the same thing to them again? Was the forgiveness that they offered conditional? Write out the story below.

_____
_____
_____
_____
_____
_____
_____
_____
_____
_____
_____
_____
_____
_____
_____

Salvation & Repentance
Section Two

Last week in the first Section of this Block, you learnt about Sin & Law. As your challenge, you were asked a set of questions about your past sins, which ones you have broken and how you may have tried to reconcile with God. The important point of the exercise was to understand that we have all broken the Law. Sometimes we may have said, 'that's just who I am', but I hope that you may have realised by the end of the exercise that God has broken the power that sin once held over us.

In this Section, we will be building upon on that information to explore the topic of salvation and repentance. We can define salvation as the 'preservation or deliverance from harm, ruin, or loss'[6]. When we talked about Law, we came to understand that the Law applies to us and condemns us. Therefore, finding deliverance from that condemnation is what we will be discussing amongst other things. Firstly, we will look at how a person can receive that personal salvation. Secondly, we will move on to learn about repentance as it is a vital component of Christian-living. You should know these topics in detail so that you can easily express your knowledge to others whenever the situations arise for you to share your faith.

Many new believers or people seeking answers about God want to know the answer to the question, 'what must I do to be saved?' Before we go into what the scriptures say about this, please make a note of what you currently believe.

---

[6] Online definitions https://www.google.ie/?gws_rd=ssl#q=definition+salvation accessed June 2016

What would you define Salvation as?

_____
_____
_____

What are the conditions of Salvation? i.e. the steps to getting saved.

_____
_____
_____

Do you consider yourself as being saved from your sin?

_____

Now, look up this verse and write it out below: **John 3:16**

_____
_____
_____

Some people declare falsely that Jesus was a failure, coming down to us where we overcame Him and put Him to death. The truth is that Jesus knew that He would die. He was choosing to give up His life and pay for our punishment willingly. Think of it this way, we were guilty of sin and were due to come before the judge at an appointed time. The judge is just, and so He was going to convict us, but Jesus stepped-in to pay the sentence for us. However, we must still accept that payment. God has offered His salvation to everyone, but sadly many people have no interest and have refused Him.

For those who have chosen to accept His sacrifice, we can be sure that Jesus took all our sin and shame when He died on the cross **1 Peter 2:24**. He then rose from the dead three days later **Matthew 28:5-7**, breaking the power of sin and offering us the gift of salvation. The Bible clearly sets out the conditions for salvation, which are:
1. We must confess that we are sinners **1 John 1:9**
2. We must believe that Jesus is the Son of God **1 John 5:13**
3. We must accept the *free* gift of salvation **Ephesians 2:8-9**
4. We must believe that Jesus has risen from the dead **Romans 10:9**

This salvation is an act of God's grace, meaning, something that we did not deserve. There is nothing that we can do to earn our own salvation. Following Jesus is the only

Way that declares such a radical thing. All other religions, and even some branches of religious 'Christians', claim that good works counteract the sins committed. Imagine for a moment a murderer who is going before a judge, and he is found guilty, but he shouts out, 'oh but I helped the lady across the street, and gave money to the orphans, and always smiled at people.' Will that make him innocent of the murder? Certainly not.

We should open our eyes to what God is saying about salvation, namely that it cannot be by our works. The Bible repeatedly declares this point. For example, think of the story of Adam and Eve. After they had sinned, they tried to make themselves appear presentable by covering themselves with leaves. However, God gave them animal skins to replace the leaves. Even then, through this act, God was saying that it would take nothing less than a blood sacrifice to cover us. God supplied our perfect sacrifice when Jesus came and died for us.

If you have been trying over the years to make yourself good enough for God, now is the time to stop. There is nothing you can do that can settle your bill, except to accept the free gift of God. If you have not given your life to God or have tried to go about it in the wrong way, perhaps take a moment now to pray. Confess that you are a sinner, declaring that you believe that Jesus is the Son of God who died and rose again, and humbly accept His payment for your sins.

In making such as step, it means that we are given a new heart. We can start afresh and that means that our lives will be changed forever. It does not mean that we will never sin again. However, it does indicate that our attitude towards sin has changed. As we continue our walk with God, the Holy Spirit will highlight areas of our lives which will need change. In response, we should always submit to His will. Furthermore, because our hearts have been made new, we will begin to notice changes in our outward behaviour. These changes can become a testimony to others about what God is doing. We should always:

1. follow Jesus **John 10:27**, and take up our cross **Matthew 16:24-26**
2. love God with all our heart, mind and soul **Matthew 22:37**
3. love our neighbours as ourselves **Matthew 22:39**

Now, these things grow and develop over time. Our love for God increases over time as does our love for others. It is important here to remember that the foundation of salvation is God's love for us. It was because of the Father's love that He sent Jesus to be our Saviour. Surely then it is right to love Him with all of our hearts.

Salvation through ALL situations

When Christians traditionally think of salvation, they might typically think of Jesus bearing all our sins, of His death and resurrection, thereby saving all those who call on His name. However, salvation is not limited to just salvation from our sins, although that is undoubtedly the most significant part. Let's examine this now by looking back at a story which we covered last week.

Open your Bible and remind yourself of the story from the Book of Samuel: **1 Samuel 7:3-11**

Previously, we mentioned how Samuel used his knowledge of the Law to dramatically turn around the situation for the benefit of his nation, Israel. This event displayed God's salvation at work, exactly as is written in the Psalms:

"The LORD is near to all who call on him, to all who call on him in truth." **Psalm 145:18** ESV

Through this example, we see that God's salvation is available in our everyday lives for the situations we face. Becoming a disciple of Jesus does not mean that we will avoid challenges, troubles and difficulties. Every day, Christians around the world face hardships and our correct response is to *seek God for His help*. We can see many other examples of the people being saved in the Scriptures, such as:
- Noah and the ark **Genesis 6&7**
- The Exodus of Israel from Egypt **Exodus 14**
- David and Goliath **1 Samuel 17**

Try to think now about how many times God may have saved you, perhaps you had an illness or a car accident. Now think about how many times He may have saved your parents, and then your grandparents, and then your great-grandparents. How many times has the intervention of God's salvation occurred in those generations to enable you to exist? This concept is a humbling thing to think about. Recognising God for all these things that He has done for you and thanking Him is a life-changing decision. Previously, we may have praised a doctor who knew what to do in an emergency, but now we should recognise the wisdom that God gave to the doctor. Previously, we might have been thankful to our boss who gave out pay rises, but now we can acknowledge that God orchestrated it. Indeed, the more we submit to God, the more He will help us.

"In all thy ways acknowledge him, and he shall direct thy paths" **Proverbs 3:6** KJV

The word salvation appears in three different tenses in the New Testament: the present perfect tense, the past tense, and the future tense. I think we need to understand salvation in these three ways. One example you could use to envisage this is Noah's Ark. The Ark was built to perfection. God gave specific dimensions and instructions for Noah to make the boat **Genesis 6:15-16**. Let this represent the future tense expression of salvation – 'you will be saved'. Secondly, a day came where Noah had to enter the Ark as the flood began **Genesis 7:6-7**. This imagery represents the past tense – 'I was saved' – which occurred at a particular point in time. Lastly, even though Noah was on a perfect Ark and had his initial day of salvation, he faced an ongoing salvation with the hope of the final day where he would find dry land **Genesis 8:6-13**. Let this represent the present perfect tense 'I am being saved'. So, we see three aspects of salvation:

- You will be saved (in the future) **Romans 10:9, Mark 16:16**
- You were saved (at a specific time) **Titus 3:4-5**
- You are being saved (day by day) **1 Corinthians 15:1-2, Ephesians 2:8**

Now let's apply these three aspects to our understanding of Jesus. Firstly, Jesus was the perfect sacrifice, planned in advance and His life was completed to perfection. When we came to know Him and met the conditions of salvation, we were saved. Secondly, there is the ongoing salvation every day of our lives. Thirdly, Jesus has promised that He will return to us and that we have the hope of resurrection. Many Christians entirely miss out on the ongoing salvation – when we are sick Jesus is our salvation, when we are in trouble Jesus is our refuge, when we are in need Jesus is our provider.

Is there any other way to salvation?

Some people believe that there are other ways to God. However, you will find that many of these beliefs reject the idea that Jesus is the Son of God, and therefore they cannot meet the requirements of salvation. On the other hand, could the Jews perhaps be saved by observing the 613 commandments of the Law of Moses? Perhaps they could. However, it is impossible for any man to obey the Law of Moses. Jesus was the only one who fulfilled the law.

What does the Bible say about other paths to salvation?

Look up this verse and write it out below: **John 14:6**

_____
_____
_____

This verse states that Jesus is the ONLY way, which utterly discounts any alternative claims. Furthermore, Jesus taught that we must be born again to see the Kingdom of God **John 3:3**.

Some people get confused about what it means to be 'born again'. It does not refer to a physical re-birth, but instead to a spiritual rebirth. You could, for example say, it is like a seed, the seed must go into the ground and die before the new life can begin as a plant. This is, of course, being true for those who truly follow Jesus. Our old-self is replaced, and we should be claiming as Paul did that – it is no longer I who live but Christ in me **Galatians 2:20.** Indeed, the old has gone the new has come **2 Corinthians 5:17** and we must take up our cross daily **Luke 9:23**, which means to put aside our own life and live for Jesus.

Can people lose their salvation?

Do you think that there is a way to lose your salvation? Answer yes or no.

_____

Imagine for a moment that you are eighteen years old and there is a person who is romantically interested in you. One evening when you were both out for dinner, you bump into a family member of theirs, and your date described you as just a 'friend'. Furthermore, for several dates, this person has always turned up late. Sometimes you thought that you had been stood up. Whenever you talk about a relationship and life plans, they share their stories of mistreatment by their parents, and so they never want to marry or have children. Whenever they speak of it, they get angry and are in a bad mood for the rest of the evening, sometimes acting out in anger. You have also noticed that this person likes to talk a lot about themselves, never really allowing you to voice your opinion, and when you do, it is completely ignored. This person has today told you that they love you, but does it sound like a person that does?

In the same way, many people appear to be Christians, but in their heart, they are just like the suitor in the story above and not lovingly treating Jesus. Jesus taught about these kinds of people and what His opinion of them are. They may claim to be saved or to be a Christian, but that might not be true. Take some time to read the four sections of Scripture listed below, then return here and continue.

Are you saved:
- A. If you deny Jesus **Matthew 10:33**
- B. If you are a lazy servant **Matthew 25:14-30**
- C. If you have unforgiveness towards others **Matthew 18:21-35**
- D. If you do not obey God, and if you do not know Jesus **Matthew 7:21-23**

You will notice that each one of these examples undermines love. If you deny Jesus, then you do not love Him. If you are a lazy servant, then you are not doing what Jesus has asked you to do. If you have unforgiveness towards others, then you do not love your neighbour. Maybe this is why Paul taught the Philippians to *'work out your salvation with fear and trembling'* **Philippians 2:12** KJV.

Ezekiel prophesied saying:

> *"But when a righteous person turns away from his righteousness and does injustice and does the same abominations that the wicked person does, shall he live? None of the righteous deeds that he has done shall be remembered; for the treachery of which he is guilty and the sin he has committed, for them he shall die"* **Ezekiel 18:24** ESV

Quite often people have misunderstood the meaning of 'grace'. Indeed, we have a grace upon us because of the righteousness of Jesus Christ. When Jesus paid for our sins, He paid for all our sin – past, present, and future. However, that does not mean that we should rush into living in sin. God has given us freedom, that freedom is not freedom to sin, but rather a *freedom from sin*. To answer 'can a person lose their salvation' I would have to say no. Examples of salvation such as the one we used of Noah, point to the coming salvation of Jesus. Noah was 'sealed' in the ark **Genesis 7:16**. He could not get out, even if he wanted to. However, if a person has rejected Jesus and is a lazy servant and has unforgiveness and does not obey God, then perhaps they were never saved in the first place. In Section Three, we will be learning all about grace and sanctification so we will be discussing these things in more detail then.

Repentance

In your opinion, what is the difference between confessing a sin, and repenting from that sin?

_____
_____
_____

Of course, to confess means to admit that God is holy and has a right to judge us, and secondly that we must admit our blame in committing sins. To repent takes us a bit further. Repentance means that we must confess what we have done wrong, expressing sincere regret, and then turning to God's way and away from that sin for good. It is a military term meaning 'about turn'. Repentance declares 'I will never do that again', whereas confession means 'oops I did it again'.

Quite a lot of people get hung up on this issue as they feel that sin has too much of a stronghold over them. We must remember that Jesus has broken the power of sin **Romans 8:2**. Not only that, but He can guide us in how to overcome the sin. Sometimes we might feel like we can't give up a specific sin and are feeling guilty (God is convicting your heart). In such situations, just pray honestly to God and say, 'Lord, I want to give up this sin and turn to You Jesus, will you help me and show me how?' If you call on Him, He will surely help **Psalm 145:18.**

Now, turn to our YouTube page and watch **discipleship training, Video 3**

If you go to our YouTube channel 'Revival Well' and then go to our Playlists, you will find one called 'Discipleship Course'. In that Playlist, you will see all the videos relating this course. Click on the one called 'Video3. I have decided. Repentance.' Alternatively, you can view or download the video directly from Google Drive at this link:

https://drive.google.com/open?id=1hUtub8yUfxczn6awBeqm3qSu7w4zICIA

Having considered the topic of repentance, in your own words, why do we need to repent to God?

_____
_____
_____

Firstly, I would say that we must remember that we are not dealing with a stone tablet with written rules. We are dealing with a person, Jesus Christ. Think for a moment about your relationship with a close friend that you have. Would they ever accept an apology from you that wasn't heartfelt? How much more then, do we need to express our remorse to Jesus, when He knows our hearts and can see any contempt, lying or deception.

SECTION TWO CHALLENGE

Now, turn to our YouTube page and watch **discipleship training, Video 4**

If you go to our YouTube channel 'Revival Well' and then go to our Playlists, you will find one called 'Discipleship Course'. In that Playlist, you will see all the videos relating this course. Click on the one called 'Video4. I have decided. Go' Alternatively, you can view or download the video directly from Google Drive at this link:

https://drive.google.com/open?id=1hUtub8yUfxczn6awBeqm3qSu7w4zICIA

Write out a sixty-second version of your testimony of how Jesus saved you. Divide it down into three parts: take twenty seconds to talk about how you used to be, another twenty seconds to talk about how God changed you and for the final twenty seconds talk about how you are now. With that done, now try as best as you can to memorise this testimony.

Your challenge for this week is this: to pray every day and to ask God for opportunities to share your testimony. Then wait, watch and be ready for those opportunities. It might end up being a chat with someone at school or at work or perhaps even someone in the shopping queue behind you. Just start off the conversation by something like, "would you like to hear a quick story?" Don't add anything on to the end of your testimony such as 'come to my church on Sunday', or anything like that. Just give them your story, that's all. Obviously, if they ask you anything after you share it with them, try to answer the questions as best as you can.

Make some notes here about how it went. What did you learn? Did you do anything or say anything that you would change the next time around?

Grace & Sanctification
Section Three

Welcome to the last Section of this Block. Over the last two weeks, you have been learning about God, about God's Laws, about sin, about salvation, and about repentance. This week, we will build upon those topics as we begin to shift toward the next Block of this course which has a focal point on maintaining a good relationship with God. Before we get there, we need to gain a better understanding of grace and sanctification. Indeed, if you have an incorrect view of these two things, then it could inadvertently affect your relationship with God.

As your challenge last week, you were set with the task of making a version of your testimony, praying to ask God for opportunities, and then actively using any chance that arises. How do you feel you got on with this? Many of us find the idea of talking to people about God as daunting. Others may have had a busy schedule and didn't get the opportunity at all. Others may have taken it in your stride, but lacked enough background to answer questions that people asked afterwards. These things are quite common so do not worry. What you need to do now, is to recognise your area of weakness, whether it is boldness, time constraints, or lack of knowledge, and commit them to God and ask Him to help you. Take some time now to pray about this, so that you can face similar challenges ahead, knowing that God will help you.

Now, turn to our YouTube page and watch **discipleship training, Video 5**

If you go to our YouTube channel 'Revival Well' and then go to our Playlists, you will find one called 'Discipleship Course'. In that Playlist, you will see all the videos relating this course. Click on the one called 'Video5. I have decided. Father.' Alternatively, you can view or download the video directly from Google Drive at this link:

https://drive.google.com/open?id=1hUtub8yUfxczn6awBeqm3qSu7w4zICIA

In the Old Testament, lambs were prepared and burnt on the altar by the priest, making atonement for sins that had been committed. Open your Bible and read **Leviticus 4:35**.

Why do you think they made these sacrifices?

_____
_____
_____

Under the Law of Moses, these sacrifices were required. One recent scientific discovery that grabbed my attention was in quantum physics. It explains that when an atom is changing, specifically when the electrons are changing position, they must first communicate that change with every other atom in the universe. You may wonder what the relevance is. Think about the priests burning the sacrifice at the altar. As that wood was set on fire, the atoms begin changing. Therefore, any sacrifice burnt with fire is communicated to the whole Universe.

Of course, in the New Testament we come to understand that these sacrifices were always pointing towards the coming Messiah, Jesus:

> "Indeed, under the law almost everything is purified with blood, and without the shedding of blood there is no forgiveness of sins" **Hebrews 9:22** ESV

In your own words, explain what was different between the old-style sacrifice of the lamb, and the sacrifice that Jesus made for us:

_____
_____
_____

Write down these verses below: **Hebrews 10:11-14**

_____
_____
_____
_____
_____
_____
_____
_____

What we learn here is that the old-style sacrifices didn't take away sin. They may have cleansed the person, but it didn't stop that person from going out again and sinning that very same day. In some sense, it was like paying a Mastercard bill. You run up a big bill and when you get notified by your monthly statement, you rush out to pay the minimum amount. Straight after which, you calculate how you spend again and the debt is never cleared.

However, when Jesus became a sacrifice for our sin, it was a one-time sacrifice for our sins. Jesus not only paid the debt that we owed, but He offers us a way to overcome the sin. We are broken from our yoke of slavery to sin.

Notice also that in **verse 14** it says that Jesus has made us perfect! In fact, we are made perfect forever! Isn't that good news that we are saved from failing to reach the standard of the Law because Jesus has fulfilled the Law on our behalf. However, even though we are made perfect, we are still undergoing a process of sanctification. **Verse 14** which states our perfection, also states and we are *'being made holy'*. That doesn't sound like a completed job. It sounds like an ongoing job.

Many people get confused at this point. Are we holy now? If so, then why do I need to be sanctified? The answer is that we have received a new spirit which is holy and righteous. However, we have not received a new mind and body. So now the two are battling with each other for supremacy. 'Sanctification' then, is the process by which the Holy Spirit makes us aware of things in us which are not holy and require change. Our response, which is to allow the Holy Spirit to change us, is a love offering.

For example, before a person turned to Jesus, they used to watch a lot of horror movies. Now, whenever one is being broadcast on TV, their flesh says 'yay' but in their heart, they don't feel comfortable. So they seek God about it. The Holy Spirit may then lead them to get rid of any horror films they own and indeed, they might be asked never to watch one ever again. These kinds of challenges are difficult for the flesh to accept, but we are called to walk by the Spirit.

Now, can you also point out what was similar between the old-style sacrifice of the lamb, and the sacrifice that Jesus made for us?

_____
_____
_____

Many people do not realise the similarities between the Passover sacrifice and the sacrifice that Jesus made at Passover. Here are some amazing similarities:

- The lamb for the Passover sacrifice is chosen five days beforehand. Jesus entered the city five days before being crucified.
- The lamb had to be male without defect. Jesus was without sin.
- The lamb must enter the City of Jerusalem by the Beautiful Gate. Jesus entered through this gate.
- At the feast of unleavened bread, you must eat pure bread (without yeast). Jesus told his followers that 'I am the Bread of Life'.
- The lamb is sacrificed at 3 o'clock. That is the exact time Jesus cried out 'it is finished'.

We see here that when Jesus came to Jerusalem to lay down His life, He became the perfect Lamb of God:

> "He was oppressed, and he was afflicted, yet he opened not his mouth; like a lamb that is led to the slaughter, and like a sheep that before its shearers is silent, so he opened not his mouth" **Isaiah 53:7 ESV.**

This raises a question which I think we should look at briefly. What do you think happened to all the people, the Israelites and Gentiles, who came before Jesus was born? Do you think they will be in heaven? Write out your thoughts here:

_____
_____
_____

There are various theories about this. I believe that we need to accept that the sacrifice provided for Abraham, and then later during the Passover in Egypt and all the sacrifices since, all point to Jesus coming as the Lamb of God. When the Ark of the Covenant was made, it was sprinkled with the blood from the lamb, but this mirrored what was going to take place in heaven, that Jesus' blood would be shed for us all. Therefore, through faith in God and His instructions they were saved. Abraham's faith was accredited to him as righteousness **Genesis 15:6**. They didn't need to understand that Jesus was coming, although some of the prophets did prophesy about Him.

Now, turn to our YouTube page and watch **discipleship training, Video 6**, which talks about sacrifice, atonement and Jesus as our Passover.

If you go to our YouTube channel 'Revival Well' and then go to our Playlists, you will find one called 'Discipleship Course'. In that Playlist, you will see all the videos relating this course. Click on the one called 'Video6. I have decided. Passover' Alternatively, you can view or download the video directly from Google Drive at this link:

https://drive.google.com/open?id=1hUtub8yUfxczn6awBeqm3qSu7w4zICIA

Let's move on to look at grace. In your own words, have a go of explaining what grace means:

_____
_____
_____

There are two main meanings of grace. In the Old Testament, we find the [Hebrew] word 'chesed' being used for grace. Chesed speaks of deliverance from enemies, afflictions and adversity. It also means enablement, daily guidance, forgiveness and preservation. In the New Testament, we find a different [Greek] word 'charis' which simply means the provision of salvation.

Therefore, grace is not a rule which enables believers to continue sinning as they please. Instead, it is a part of our daily walk with God - indeed something which we do not deserve. However, many Christians use grace as an excuse to continue sinning.

What is your opinion on the matter?

_____
_____
_____

You will remember from Section Two that we took time to look at types of situations where some people claimed to be saved, but were instead not going to reach heaven at all.

Knowledge Challenge #2 [Answer on page 114]

Which of the below options sound right to you? Find a Bible verse to support your answer:

A. Jesus died and has forgiven my past sins and future sins, every time I sin, I can simply go to Him and ask forgiveness.
B. Jesus died and has forgiven my past sins and set me free from any desire to sin but if I do happen to sin then I lose my salvation.
C. Jesus died and has forgiven my past sins and future sins, so I do not need to worry about if I sin or not.
D. Jesus died and has forgiven my past sins and has set me free from my desire to sin, but if I do happen to sin, I should discuss it with Jesus, repent and to find out how to conquer the enemies' hold over me in that area, so that the enemy and the sin can be overcome.

Your answer A B C or D:

_____

Now look up these following verses and write them out:

Galatians 5:1

_____
_____
_____

1 Peter 2:16

_____
_____
_____

Romans 6:18

_____
_____
_____

Romans 8:1

_____
_____

Romans 6:22

We were slaves but now we are made free from sin and have exchanged that slavery for another, to be slaves to righteousness, becoming more holy. We have gained eternal life.

Now, turn to our YouTube page and watch **discipleship training, Video 7**

If you go to our YouTube channel 'Revival Well' and then go to our Playlists, you will find one called 'Discipleship Course'. In that Playlist, you will see all the videos relating this course. Click on the one called 'Video7. I have decided. The Word.' Alternatively, you can view or download the video directly from Google Drive at this link:

https://drive.google.com/open?id=1hUtub8yUfxczn6awBeqm3qSu7w4zICIA

What do you think the word sanctification means? Write your thoughts here:

In Section Two, we mentioned what the life of a believer should look like: to take up our cross daily, laying aside our own lives and allowing our minds to be renewed. It means that as time proceeds we should move towards being completely sanctified. This is outlined by Paul who wrote:

> *"Now may the God of peace himself sanctify you completely, and may your whole spirit and soul and body be kept blameless at the coming of our Lord Jesus Christ"* **1 Thessalonians 5:23** ESV.

Sanctification follows a standard process. Central to this process is the work of the Holy Spirit. Many Christians associate the Holy Spirit with the gifts of the Holy Spirit, mighty miracles, revivals and powerful worship. That is not the focus of the Holy Spirit. Out of all the possible names in the Universe, God the Father chose to call the Spirit the Holy

Spirit. The focus of the Holy Spirit is to bring us into holiness through the process of sanctification. People experiencing gifts and miracles is what naturally occurs when we are walking humbly with God with a loving heart.

The process of sanctification happens like this:

The Holy Spirit convicts us of a specific sin we are committing. We are to respond to this by repenting of that sin and never returning to it. This step means that we have given up another piece of our old selves and become more like Jesus. This process should be an ongoing process no matter what level of ministry you are in, no matter how long you have been walking with Jesus. In this process, we must remember that *"For whom the Lord loves He corrects, even as a father corrects the son in whom he delights"* **Proverbs 3:12** AMP. Many people forget that sanctification is another way in which God reveals His love to us. We should be running to Him eager to give up more, rather than complaining that we must give something up.

One of the most common mistakes is the belief that we must strive and strain to take ourselves through the sanctification process. However, Apostle Paul declared that just as salvation is by faith, so is sanctification **Galatians 2:17-21**. Yes, we must be willing participants in the process, but we cannot use the circumstances to mock others who have not yet repented. Instead, a humble hearted disciple weeps and prays for people who are continuing in their sin.

Let's answer two important questions about sanctification:

What happens if I was convicted of a sin by the Holy Spirit, but I didn't do anything about it? What quite often happens in these cases is nothing. There could be a silence from God until you have tackled your sin, your worship time and Bible study time might just feel empty until you sort out the sin and repent. However, things can be even worse than just silence. Sometimes, if we have let the issue go too far, an emergency/dramatic situation might occur to shake us up. Let's just say, that the longer we leave it, the worse it will get. But God is faithful, and if you have run away from sanctification, it is not too late to turn back to Him, to repent to the Holy Spirit for not listening and to repent of the sin and never look back.

I was convicted of a sin and repented, but my brother in the Lord is committing that same sin openly and not doing anything about it. What should I do? You need to step carefully. The Holy Spirit convicts each person at different points in their walk. Indeed, the sanctification process is by faith and not by law. For example, imagine two believers at the same age, one is convicted for drinking habits at twenty-five, but the other is not convicted of the same sin until the age of forty. It would be easy for the twenty-five-year-old to turn and judge the other person. But at that time the Holy Spirit could have been challenging the other person regarding different sins. We are not to be judges. Only God is a righteous judge. What is important is to see that the person loves God with all their heart and is actively going through sanctification. If you feel that they are not, and that they need to be corrected, the Bible sets out the process by which we can correct and challenge each other **Matthew 18:15-17, 1 Corinthians 5:9-13**. But be wary. Any such move should be done with love **Galatians 6**.

Take five to ten minutes in prayer to seek God. Ask the Holy Spirit to remind you of any sin that you were convicted of but ignored. Use this opportunity to mend your relationship with Jesus and to ensure that the sanctification process is renewed and running as it should do once more.

SECTION THREE CHALLENGE

In this week's challenge, you are going to be asked a set of challenging questions which focus on your relationship with God. This is aimed at preparing you for the next Block of three weeks where we will be focusing on your relationship with God.

How much time do you think a person should spend with God every day? Are you currently spending this amount of time with God?

_____
_____
_____
_____

Are there any specific things that distract you from spending time with God? List them:

_____
_____
_____
_____

Have you got a place/space where you know you can go to, to have quality time with God? Where is it? What do you normally do for your daily devotion - worship / prayer / study?

_____
_____

_____
_____

How do you feel if you miss your daily devotion time?

_____
_____
_____
_____

Are there other times of the day, other than your daily devotion where you spend time in prayer?

_____
_____
_____
_____

Out of all the activities that you do, are there any that have a negative influence on your mood / personality / time? What are they - list them.

_____
_____
_____
_____

How should we treat things that distract us from God?

Write out this verse: **Matthew 5:29**

_____
_____
_____
_____

I HAVE DECIDED

There are 268 hours in a week. Using the chart below, try to work out how you spend every hour of the week:

Activities:	Number of hours per week:
Working	
Housework & cleaning	
Watching TV	
Personal prayer time	
Sleeping	
Driving / travelling	
Study (school/college)	
Reading (non-Christian books)	
Time allocated to worship God	
Shopping	
Exercise	
Church events & fellowship	
Entertaining guests	
Quality time with friends	
Quality time with partner	
Quality time with family	
Eating	
Personal Bible study	
Other activities	
Remaining Unknown hours	

Hearing from God
Section Four

Welcome to the second Block of Sections, for the next three weeks we are going to look at your relationship with God. For the last three Sections, we have covered Sin & Law, Salvation & Repentance, and Grace & Sanctification. There is a reason why we have looked at those topics before looking at how we get closer to God. Firstly, we must be saved. Secondly, we must ensure that we are being sanctified and allowing the Holy Spirit to change us on an ongoing basis. These basics set us on the right path to getting closer to God. This Section will focus on how we hear from God. If you want to be able to hear the voice of God, you must be maintaining that loving relationship with Jesus.

As your challenge last week, you were asked a set of questions about how you spend your time. This request will hopefully have got you thinking about whether you have put God as the number one priority in your life. Hopefully, you will have realised some areas where you could reduce distractions and focus on God. Whether it is by watching less TV or less surfing on your Facebook feed, making a dedication to God to spend more time with Him is vital. Take some time now to ask God to help you set aside more time for Him. Ask Him to help you overcome the distractions that you face.

You cannot rush a relationship. If you feel that you need to spend more time seeking Jesus to restore that relationship and to restore the sanctification process, then do that before moving any further.

Once again, we will start by looking at the life of Samuel. Open your Bible and read **1 Samuel 3:2-14**, and answer the following questions:

I HAVE DECIDED

Who was God speaking to?

___

Did Eli know it was possible for God to speak?

___

Why do you think that Eli couldn't hear God's voice?

___

What did God say to Samuel?

___

Why was Eli to be punished?

___

Do you think Eli's lack of obedience/lack of repentance/lack of correction has anything to do with his inability to hear God's voice? Write your thoughts:

___

___

___

Now, turn to our YouTube page and watch **discipleship training, Video 8**

If you go to our YouTube channel 'Revival Well' and then go to our Playlists, you will find one called 'Discipleship Course'. In that Playlist, you will see all the videos relating this course. Click on the one called 'Video8. I have decided. Prayer.' Alternatively, you can view or download the video directly from Google Drive at this link:

> https://drive.google.com/open?id=1hUtub8yUfxczn6awBeqm3qSu7w4zICIA

In the Bible, we find many examples of people hearing from God and either acting in obedience or disobedience. Can you think of any examples?

New Testament:

___

Old Testament:

One example of obedience from the New Testament is Ananias who went to find Saul to pray with him, see **Acts 9:17-18**. An Example of obedience from the Old Testament would be Amos, see **Amos 1:1-2**. Many of the Old Testament prophets were people who just heard the words of God, obeyed and spoke what they were told to speak. For many modern Christians, the idea that God can speak to us is a foreign concept.

Perhaps this attitude towards 'hearing voices' comes from the era where such people were locked away in asylums. Many churches teach that the Bible is the only way to hear God's words. In other churches, some 'special' speakers declare God's Words to people in a prophetic manner. In other cases, some speakers declare words as coming from God, when they haven't at all - we can call such people false prophets. Jeremiah faced false prophets in his day, and he spoke of God's opinion of them, saying *"I have not sent these prophets, yet they ran: I have not spoken to them, yet they prophesied. But if they had stood in my counsel, and had caused my people to hear my words, then they should have turned them from their evil way, and from the evil of their doings"* **Jeremiah 23:21-22** KJV.

The reason why so many people flock to hear men and women who call themselves prophets, is because they do not personally know how to hear God. Herein lies a huge problem, if we don't hear God, then we will walk blindly. There are many Christians who want to walk the right path but make the wrong decisions simply because they don't know how to hear from God. 'Hearing God's voice' is not a sermon topic that I have ever heard, but it is probably one of the most important teachings because without God's voice we don't have His wisdom and direction. If we, as Christians reject the idea of hearing God's voice, we would be like the people that Hosea spoke of when he said, *"My people are destroyed for lack of knowledge"* **Hosea 4:6a** AMP.

What you might find shocking, is that the days where people will not hear the words of the Lord was prophesied by Amos:

> *"Behold, the days are coming, says the Lord God, when I will send a famine in the land, not a famine of bread, nor a thirst for water, but [a famine] for hearing the words of the Lord. And [the people] shall wander from sea to sea and from the north even to the east; they shall run to and fro to seek the word of the Lord [inquiring for and requiring it as one requires food], but shall not find it. In that day shall the fair virgins and young men faint for thirst"* **Amos 8:11-13** AMP.

Traditionally, some scholars have debated about the meaning of this passage, speculating that there would be a period where people will not be able to purchase the Bible. However, in this passage, it clearly states a famine of 'hearing the words', not a famine of 'reading the word' of God. Indeed, in countries that have historically banned Christianity, people have found it hard to purchase a Bible, such as in the Soviet Union during the days of the Cold War. However, we also know that wherever Christians are persecuted that Christianity thrives. During the years of the Soviet Union, many missionaries drove across the border with Bibles at the risk of their own lives, and many Bibles got through. God can always open closed doors.

In modern times, persecution of Christians is increasing, and it is entirely possible that online-retailers of books may prohibit selling Bibles sometime in the future. However, with an increase in technology, Bibles can now be sent by email through encryption software. So once again I make the point that this prophecy most likely refers to the time that we have been living in, where most Christians haven't had a clue about how to hear God's voice. Those days are coming to an end. Right across the world people are now beginning to know how to hear God and obey, and hopefully, by the end of this Section, you will join that number.

Let's move on. With this next set of questions, try to be as honest as possible. Don't worry if you feel that there is room for improvement!

On average, how much time do you spend in prayer in a day?

_____

Out of that amount of time, what percentage would you say is made up of requests (asking for needs etc.)?

_____

From your Bible, now read **John 1:1-5**.

In these verses, John is saying that Jesus is the Word, and the Word was there from the beginning. Jesus, the Living Word, has not stopped speaking. But have we forgotten to listen?

In your prayer times, how often do you stop talking and listen?

_____

Imagine a man called John. He has a friend called Dave who turns up at his door and proceeds to talk nonstop for three hours. Before John can say anything, Dave runs off home to boast to his other friends about the length of discussion he had with John. In the same way, there has been a recent emphasis to pray for long periods of time in one of those twenty-four-hour prayer rooms, even posting about it on social networks both during and afterwards. Are we treating God exactly like Dave is treating John?

Instead, if you were sat in your kitchen with your best friend, sharing a pot of tea, it would be reasonable to think that you would spend half the time talking and half the time listening. It would not be rushed. It would not be boasted about afterwards. The things said there would remain private unless your friend asked you to share it. Now, this is more like how we should be with God. Prayer has one purpose – it is a conversation with God. It is not supposed to be a one-sided conversation. Communication is supposed to be interactive!

Write out this verse: **1 Corinthians 14:5**

_____
_____
_____
_____
_____

What is very clear from this verse is that Paul was encouraging every believer to prophesy. Why do you think he would do that?

_____
_____
_____

As mentioned before, prophecy is simply hearing the Word of God and speaking it forth or acting in obedience to what was heard. If every believer could do this efficiently, we would become spiritually mature and be less prone to deception by the devil. Instead, we would be allowing God to establish our steps – *"The steps of a man are established by the Lord, when he delights in his way"* **Psalms 37:23** ESV.

What do you think God sounds like when He speaks to us? Write your thoughts here:

_____
_____
_____

When I was younger, I thought that when God spoke it would be like this: I would be standing on top of a mountain, a huge cloud would gather around the summit and engulf me in a heavy fog. Then there would be a great light and out from the cloud would speak a voice that was so deep and loud that even the very ground would shake. Of course, God could speak to us this way, but it is likely that perhaps Moses might be one of the few to ever experience this. Elijah on the other hand, had a completely different experience:

> *"And He said, go out and stand on the mount before the Lord. And behold, the Lord passed by, and a great and strong wind rent the mountains and broke in pieces the rocks before the Lord, but the Lord was not in the wind; and after the wind an earthquake, but the Lord was not in the earthquake; And after the earthquake a fire, but the Lord was not in the fire; and after the fire [a sound of gentle stillness and] a still, small voice. When Elijah heard the voice, he wrapped his face in his mantle and went out and stood in the entrance of the cave. And behold, there came a voice to him and said, what are you doing here, Elijah?"* **1 Kings 19:11-13** AMP.

For Elijah, when he heard God, it was a "still, small voice". Herein lies a problem. If the voice of God is a still, small voice, then how can we tell the difference between that sound and any other voices/thoughts?

The answer is that we must be able to discern which voice we are hearing.

Our own voice – Our consciousness tends to have motives. For example, a man who is in love with the wrong girl might go to the Bible for guidance. His personal feelings may overpower him and guide him to read verses of confirmation rather than understanding what God is saying. Our motives quite often do not line up with scripture. Therefore, our first line of defence is knowing the Bible. Our second line of protection is to seek council with a mentor or pastor to see if their Biblical opinion is in-line with our conclusion.

The devil's voice – the devil is always trying to pull us down, quite often he uses lies that are contrary to the promises that God has spoken over us. However, the devil also knows scripture and may use small portions of it to distort our thinking incorrectly. For example, imagine a man called John, a drunk driver has knocked down and killed his brother Dave. John goes to the Bible looking for answers, but the devil grabs hold of the anger in his heart and guides him to think of the Law, an eye for an eye, a tooth for a tooth **Exodus 21:24**. John goes out and gets a knife and stabs the man who killed his brother. In this case, John lacked a good foundational knowledge of the Bible, such as being told to turn the other cheek **Matthew 5:38-42**. Once again, our protection is having an extensive understanding of scripture.

I cannot express enough the importance of reading your Bible. Over time, we do become more discerning. Perhaps we get it wrong sometimes, but the point is, to keep trying and asking God to guide us.

God's voice – as believers in our era, we have a great advantage, in that God speaks to us through the Holy Spirit. So, we should hear words spoken into our hearts. We must always be discerning and check that it lines up with a diverse range of scriptures. We could also ask God to send an independent person to us with a word of confirmation. We can also test it by fulfilment. God's words to us are not empty words - *"so shall my word be that goes out from my mouth; it shall not return to me empty, but it shall accomplish that which I purpose, and shall succeed in the thing for which I sent it"* **Isaiah 55:11** ESV.

Discernment: How do I tell if a person can prophesy?

If a person prophesies an edifying word, then it must come true, if not then they weren't speaking words from God but from their own mind **Deuteronomy 18:22**. If a person prophesies correction/rebuke/disaster, the hope is that the person/people will turn to God and away from disaster. The goal is not fulfillment but rather repentance and mercy. That is more difficult to discern, but not impossible. The main point of discernment is this, is the person humble? If a person claims to be a prophet and sits around listening to people say how great they are without rejecting them, you will need to be worried. But if the person shies away from official titles and the limelight, then listen to their words! Without a humble heart, a prophet cannot clearly hear the words of God, nor indeed can any of us.

Returning to how God speaks to us, there are a variety of ways which He can guide us:
- With a gentle whisper **1 Kings 19:11-13**
- While speaking in tongues **Romans 8:26-27**
- Through visions **Acts 2:17**
- Through dreams **Acts 2:17**
- Through the Bible **2 Timothy 3:16**

I would like to pause for a moment before we look at the steps to hearing God's voice. We must bring love into the equation. Paul taught us this – *"If I speak in the tongues of men and of angels, but have not love, I am a noisy gong or a clanging cymbal. And if I have prophetic powers, and understand all mysteries and all knowledge, and if I have all faith, so as to remove mountains, but have not love, I am nothing"* **1 Corinthians 13:1-2** ESV. We should also consider that *"And if I have prophetic powers, and understand all mysteries and all knowledge, and if I have all faith, so as to remove mountains, but have not love, I am nothing"* **James 3:17** KJV.

What this means for us is that when we hear God's voice and gain wisdom from heaven that we don't go and use it in an ungodly way. For example, a few years ago I was at a meeting where there was a visiting worship leader. As he played, I felt that the Holy Spirit was telling me that his songs weren't personal enough, and they indeed were not on a one-to-one basis with God. Now the Holy Spirit wanted me to say something to him, but I had options. I could have gone up and said, 'God told me to say all your songs are no good.' That would have immediately sparked a defensive position and a 'who do you think you are' moment. We can hear from God, but that doesn't mean that I can deliver the message anyway that I see fit. Love is always the goal, so that people are brought closer to God. If we do it in the wrong manner, then the message is likely to be rejected! In this case, I said to him, 'God has some new songs that He wants you to write with Him.' He was blessed, and my words were accepted. We should understand that we are not perfect vessels for what the Holy Spirit is trying to do and say through us. We get things wrong from time to time. It might be a faulty interpretation or even just a misplaced word. The most important thing to remember is to be loving to those around you.

The steps to hearing God's voice

There are many different places in the Bible to draw from and many ways which God speaks, so for this section we are going to simplify things. We are going to look at four steps to hearing God's voice, based on this scripture:

"I will stand upon my watch, and set me upon the tower, and will watch to see what he will say unto me, and what I shall answer when I am reproved. And the LORD answered me, and said, Write the vision, and make it plain upon tables, that he may run that readeth it" **Habakkuk 2:1-2** KJV.

Step One – *"I will stand at my watch"* – what this means to us is that we want to quiet ourselves in the Lord's presence. For each person, this will mean a different thing. As for me, I like to go out walking and be in the Lord's presence and listen. For another person, it might happen while swimming, or while sitting on their bed. We need to start with being quiet, allowing space and opportunity for God to speak to us.

Step Two – *"I will look to see"* – expect the Lord to speak as you wait on Him. Don't empty your mind like secular meditation, but instead fill your mind with thoughts of Jesus.

Step Three – *"what He will say to me"* – The Holy Spirit often speaks to us through our heart and these may come as words direct to our hearts, but they are not limited to just that. I have heard of people experiencing things like severe back pain, but it was God telling them to go and help a person who had that pain. Once they prayed for the person, their own pain was gone too. Another way could be the Holy Spirit guiding you to a specific Bible verse, or bring particular passages to mind as you seek Him.

Step Four – *"Then the Lord said, 'Write down the revelation"* – Write down the words, thoughts, visions and dreams that God gives you. Go out and buy a notepad and keep a journal, noting the date and what you feel God was saying to you. I have been doing this now for several years, and after a while, you can read back through your notes and get a stable picture of what God is saying to you through a season.

Now it's time for you to give it a try. Bearing the four steps in mind, I want you to go through these but rather than remaining completely quiet, I want you to ask God some specific questions, wait on Him and then write down the answer you hear. Write out what you feel is the response that God has given you:

Ask the Lord: 'Lord Jesus, as I wait on you, would you speak to me about my family Lord?'

Write down anything you hear, feel or see, or any verse that comes to mind:

_____
_____
_____

Now ask the Lord: 'Lord Jesus, as I continue to wait on you, would you speak to me about my church Lord?

Write down anything you hear, feel or see, or any verse that comes to mind:

_____
_____
_____

Finally, ask the Lord: 'Lord Jesus, I would also like to know what you want to say to me about my nation, will you speak to me and show me your heart for my nation?'

Write down anything you hear, feel or see, or any verse that comes to mind:

_____
_____
_____

So, you have had your first attempt, do not be dismayed if you find this challenging at first. Instead, be encouraged to keep seeking the Lord in this way. Make sure that you put a journal/notepad on your shopping list. Carry it with you as often as possible! Now as we have already mentioned, we need to discern what we have heard, you can do that by asking these questions about what you have just written:

- How does it compare with the character of God? (for example - Jehovah Jireh – meaning God our provider)
- How does it compare to Biblical principles? (for example – love your neighbour)
- Test the origin – ask God for a confirmation or a Bible verse.
- How does it compare to God's promises?
- You could also share what you wrote with a mentor to hear their thoughts on the matter.
- Later, you can also test the fruits of what you have written down, remembering that God's word does not return void.

SECTION FOUR CHALLENGE

Once again, the time has come to apply some of what we have been learning in a practical setting. For this week's' challenge, we want you to carry out a random act of kindness. Here are some examples of what you could do:

- Let someone go ahead of you in a queue
- Buy a chocolate bar and give it to a random person
- Befriend a person at school/college who is ostracised by others

Now before you run out your door to do this, I want you to remember to pray before you go, and remember to pray for the person afterwards. Also, if your random act of kindness leads to a conversation, look to share your sixty-second testimony with them, start by saying 'can I share something with you?'

After you have completed this challenge, make some notes about how it went. What went right? What went wrong? What can I learn from this experience for next time?

_____
_____
_____
_____
_____
_____
_____

MIKE HARPER

Intimate Prayer
Section Five

As your challenge last week, you were set with the task of doing a random act of kindness with the hope that it may lead to an opportunity of sharing your testimony with someone. How do you feel you got on with this? As previously mentioned, it is essential to take these experiences and to recognise your strengths and weaknesses. As before, take a few minutes right now to ask God to help you overcome your weaknesses so that you may grow in boldness to share with people openly and without fear. Reaching out to people should come naturally to us. Certainly, doing little things like an act of kindness may not feel comfortable at first. Imagine a person learning to play the guitar. At first, it may hurt their fingers, and they will make many mistakes before becoming fluent in music. Even though you may not see fruit at first, do not give up, just continually submit your mistakes and weaknesses to God so that He will help you the next time.

In this Section, we are going to look at how Christians pray, both as individuals and as a collective. If you have been around churches for many years, you might find some of the concepts here challenging. They say that 'people don't like change', but people repeatedly vote for change in political elections. In our spiritual walk, positive change often comes at a cost, and it is those who cannot accept the price that will refuse to change.

A great example of a change in nature is that of the eagle. When an eagle reaches an age of around forty years old, its beak and talons have grown so long that they have become ineffective. At this point, the eagle must decide, to carry on without change and slowly die of starvation, or to go through a process of change. Change requires the eagle to claw its beak off, and wait for it to grow back, and then it will bite off all its talons until they too grow back. By going through this process of change, their hunting becomes efficient and productive once again, and the eagle can carry on living till around the age of seventy.

In the same way, we must honestly ask if our personal prayer time is still effective? Is the prayer meeting at our church still active? Or has it grown cold whereby there is no display of affection? At what point should we stop and realise that we are slowly starving, and need to change? I hope that time is now – so let's move forward and look at intimate prayer.

Knowledge Challenge #3

Imagine for a moment that you have the responsibility of running the prayer meeting for your church. The prayer meeting is usually held on a Friday night from 7 pm to 8 pm. Earlier in the week, you receive an email from the pastor with the suggested prayer points for the meeting. You know from attending for many years that the group would typically cover eight prayer topics in the hour.

Look over the list of prayer requests listed below and *circle* the eight that you would choose to include in the prayer meeting this Friday:

1. John (a church member) is unwell and in hospital
2. The church evangelism is taking place on Saturday
3. A local preacher has been shot dead
4. James (a church member) needs a job
5. There is a visiting preacher coming to share on Sunday
6. 10,000 asylum seekers have arrived in the city
7. Mark and his wife (church members) have found out they are expecting a baby and have asked for prayer
8. Last Sunday there was technical sound problems
9. There is an upcoming referendum
10. Matthew's son (Matthew is a deacon of the church) is being bullied at school
11. The church requires to purchase a minibus and needs to raise funds
12. The apartments next to the church have been vandalised
13. Luke's mother (an elderly member of the church) has been diagnosed with cancer
14. The church building is too small, need to pray for a new one
15. The government plans to remove tax exemption for all churches

What influenced your choice of eight topics?

_____
_____
_____

Is there any way that all the topics could have been covered?

_____
_____
_____

Of course, there are ways to cover all the topics. You could for example, divide the people into groups and assign prayer points to them. Our point here is that sometimes we sometimes **obey the traditions** rather than looking beyond them. Let's look at another dynamic to the situation we are discussing.

The prayer meeting goes ahead as normal with the eight prayer points you have chosen. One of the members, John goes first, and followed by seven other people, each of them taking the eight prayer points that you chose. As each of the eight people pray, everyone else listens attentively and says amen at the end of their prayers. Now try to answer the following questions:

Recognising the fact that a prayer is a person-to-God conversation, if thirty people attended the meeting, how many of them have prayed-out-loud to God?

_____
_____
_____

If the prayer meeting continued for an hour, how many man-hours of prayer were covered?

_____
_____
_____

Considering thirty people were present, how many man-hours of prayer were possible if everyone was praying simultaneously?

_____

In the past, and certainly in prayer meetings that I attended in my youth, many of the meetings consisted of a similar program to the above example, a group of people sat in a circle taking turns to pray and saying amen at the end of each other's prayers. So, our point being highlighted here is that **not all prayers need corporate agreement**.

Imagine you are in school/back at school. You usually spend your lunch break with your best friend. Now imagine a boy called John who decides to walk alongside you both, listening to all your conversations. John even tries to laugh along with your jokes. In response, you have three options which are (a) to try and include John (b) you could try and avoid or hide away from John or (c) you could keep your conversation impersonal, holding back any secrets or deep conversation. In the context of prayer meetings, quite often churches have opted for option (c). In so many prayer meetings, the prayer has become impersonal because people are speaking with the knowledge that everyone is listening. People should come boldly to the throne, to weep or cry, or be joyful in the presence of God. Sadly, many people have decided to remove emotion from prayer, but do you think God is content with that?

Would it be right for a wife to remove all emotion from her conversations with her husband? To keep her words boring and bland and spoken for the entertainment of others. Certainly not.

Of course, there are times when corporate prayer is required. Such examples would be: for corporate repentance of a whole church body or nation, to pray against an enemy stronghold in a church's territory, to pray in solidarity for people in need and the list goes on. However, as you have learnt already, there must be obedience to God. So, when are we to pray as a corporate body saying amen to each other's prayers? We must do it when God tells us to.

So, what do we do for the rest of the prayer time where we are not praying corporately?

We really must challenge the idea of a prayer meeting as being a place where we can tick the box on assigned prayer points. Instead, we should focus on facilitating people to experience God.

Intimacy: We can define 'intimacy' in this context as being closely acquainted, familiar, private and personal, a very close friend.

Prayer: Some people define 'prayer' as 'a solemn request for help or expression of thanks addressed to God'[7]. However, this definition remains incomplete because it does not include any reference to a conversation. It is based on how prayer meetings have

---

[7] Online definitions https://www.google.ie/?gws_rd=ssl#q=definition+prayer accessed July 2016

existed in the past. We must understand that to pray, means to converse with God, to have a two-way conversation with Him. To spend time with Him where He will tell us secrets and mysteries and new revelations that no one else has understood before. It is an exciting thing, and not simply someone listing off their needs like a shopping list. We should never treat God like Tesco's online shopping. Yes, God does supply all our needs, but the supply of our needs is not the foundation of why He wants us to talk with Him.

Intimate prayer: Therefore, we can define 'intimate prayer' as spending personal and private time talking with God in a way that develops a close friendship with Him. Our prayer meetings should facilitate this. However, having the 'weird' third person along can ruin private time with God. As believers, we should make it a priority to spend time with God, and not let anything stand in our way of intimate prayer with God. You should never allow any person or job or hobby or even ministry get between you and your prayer life.

You may ask at this point, why are we shifting from structured prayer meetings to facilitating intimate prayer with God?

In your Bible, read **Hosea 2:9-20**

If this passage is understood in terms of God speaking to His church, why might there be a spiritual shift to intimate prayer? Write your thoughts here:

_____
_____
_____

These verses help us to consider that the Bride (the church) is preparing itself for the return of her groom (Jesus).

When we gather in His name, we should note that *"For where two or three are gathered together in my name, there am I in the midst of them"* **Matthew 18:20** KJV. This statement is not a hypothetical 'Jesus is here'. If two or three gather in Jesus name, then Jesus is there with them and they can converse with Him and listen to what He has to say. There is a level of prayer that can only be experienced in a group setting. Stop for a moment and think about whom it is that you get to talk with when you are praying! It is God, the maker of the universe and nothing is too difficult for Him **Jeremiah 32:17**.

Opposition to prayer

Now if intimate prayer is the most important thing as a disciple, then you can be sure that the devil will always try to destroy your prayer life. There are two common ways which the devil comes against our prayer life which I would like to address.

Firstly, you should never boast about your prayer life. Do not go to a 24hour prayer room, pray for 24 hours and then brag on social media about it. Do not rush onto a stage to pray so that all the people can hear what a great intercessor you are. Jesus instructed us about prayer, saying:

"And when you pray, you must not be like the hypocrites. For they love to stand and pray in the synagogues and at the street corners, that they may be seen by others. Truly, I say to you, they have received their reward" **Matthew 6:5** ESV

Secondly, the devil may attack you to accuse you of lacking enough prayer time. Let me give you an example. Imagine I went a whole week without praying and the devil came to me saying 'Oh you're such a bad Christian' or 'You are not worthy of Jesus'. This accusation is the enemy trying to evoke the same response Adam and Eve had when they ran off and hid from God. If this ever happens to you, reject what the devil is saying and go to God in prayer and admit your failures, repent and move forward. Always remember that God is there to help us improve our prayer life. He is always there to help us overcome anything that stands in the way of our prayer life, and what a beautiful prayer it is for God to hear 'Lord remove anything that stands between you and I'. So, if you lack wisdom in how to move forward with God then think about what James taught:

"If any of you lacks wisdom, let him ask God, who gives generously to all without reproach, and it will be given him" **James 1:5** ESV.

Now, turn to our YouTube page and watch **discipleship training, Video 9**

If you go to our YouTube channel 'Revival Well' and then go to our Playlists, you will find one called 'Discipleship Course'. In that Playlist, you will see all the videos relating this course. Click on the one called 'Video9. I have decided. Know God.' Alternatively, you can view or download the video directly from Google Drive at this link:

https://drive.google.com/open?id=1hUtub8yUfxczn6awBeqm3qSu7w4zICIA

When you spend time with Jesus in intimate prayer, you will be filled with an ongoing testimony of what Jesus is doing and has done in your life. Sometimes sharing these experiences with other people can be problematic. You may ask, what if people think I am crazy because I tell them about how I meet with Jesus regularly and hear His voice? This challenge has always been there. In fact, after Jesus was crucified, His disciples initially rejected the idea that they would still be able to meet with Him. In your Bible, read this passage: **Mark 16:9-14.**

A Testimony of meeting with Jesus: back in 2013, two friends and I embarked on a new journey. We met once a week and sought God. We had no set structure. We brought no set props. We had no finish time. The result was that each time we met, we had such a beautiful time with God that it is mostly unexplainable. I can tell you that through those months God changed my heart in dramatic ways. One night I decided to ask God, 'how much do you love me?' It might sound like a selfish question, seeing as though Jesus has done so much. But at the time I needed to know the application of that to my own life. Over the next couple of hours, God took me in visions to see every dark moment of my life. It was more than a vision because all of the emotions of each dark memory were being felt in my heart as I saw the scenes play out in front of me. Then, at the height of emotion, God spoke to me these words, "Even then I had a plan for you". I wept, crying in the corner of the room for hours.

Of course, because those meetings were so intense and so intimate with God, we soon increased the number of times that we were meeting. Soon we were meeting five days a week. Nobody wanted to miss it. Others came and joined us too. It was like we couldn't miss it because if we did, we would be missing out on so much that God wanted to speak to us. Jesus took priority over everything. Nothing would hold us back, not even tiredness or illness. We met in prayer and worshipped and talked about God for hours and hours – sometimes, time didn't even seem to exist. It had no bearing on us. Then, that season ended, and we all moved on. But I still remember those six months fondly. I remember every moment Jesus spent with me. I remember the words He spoke. I remember the things that He showed me. It was exciting and so very removed from my experiences of prayer meetings in my youth.

Read **1 Thessalonians 5:16-18**

Does this passage challenge you to pray more? When are we to pray? In what circumstances are we to pray? Write your thoughts here:

_____
_____
_____

SECTION FIVE CHALLENGE

For this week's challenge, you need to think about your relationship with God. The questions below will ask about love and relationships. If you need to write these on a separate piece of paper and discard afterwards, please do so.

What is unconditional love? Where does unconditional love come from? Read **1 John 4:15-19**

_____
_____
_____
_____

What are your favourite Bible verses that show the love of God? [For example, **John 3:16**]

_____
_____
_____
_____

How do you feel that God expresses His love to you? For example - by being faithful. List a Bible verse which matches how you feel.

_____
_____
_____
_____

How does God's faithfulness compare to that of family & friends? Read **Psalm 86:15-17**

_____
_____
_____
_____

How does God's love compare to that of your friends? Read **1 Corinthians 13:4-7**

_____
_____
_____
_____

I HAVE DECIDED

List out the ten most important people (friends, family etc.) in your life. Rate them from 1 to 10, 1 being the most important, and 10 being the least important. For convenience, you can list both parents on the same line, and you can also list all your children on the same line.

Person:	Rate relationship importance from 1 to 10

Where should Jesus be placed in our priorities? Read **Luke 14:26**

_____
_____
_____
_____
_____
_____
_____

If God is our priority, sometimes we must sacrifice enough time to spend with Him that we would have normally spent with friends and family. Can you point out any difficulties that this might cause? Can you explain any benefits of quality time with God?

Intimate Worship
Section Six

As your challenge last week, you were asked a set of questions aimed at identifying where God stands in your priorities. At first, you may have asked, how do I sacrifice family time to be with God? However, we must realise how much we need God! By spending quality time with God, we should be overflowing with His love and with the fruit of the Spirit. That, in turn, will help to improve your relationships with others. Think about it. Imagine a husband who dedicates 100% of his time (outside work) to his wife's demands, but in doing so, he is cold, cranky, short-tempered and not pleasant to be around. Imagine now a different husband who still gives 90% of his time to his wife, but 10% to God. As a result, he is always kind, loving, and pleasant to be around. Would you prefer the 100% or the 90%? This basic illustration shows how you can set God as your number one priority. Take some time now to ask God to help you set aside more time for Him, and to help you improve any other close relationships with people. Ask Him to help you to be more loving and to fill you with the fruit of the Spirit **Galatians 5:22-23**.

In this Section, we will be discussing the topic of worship. Many Christians associate worship with just singing songs. As we will discover in this Section, worship encompasses much more than that. Indirectly, we touched upon this topic in Section Three when we discussed living a life of sanctification. Worship is a way of life. Apostle Paul wrote, saying *"I appeal to you therefore, brothers, by the mercies of God, to present your bodies as a living sacrifice, holy and acceptable to God, which is your spiritual worship"* **Romans 12:1** ESV.

As we have already discussed that context, in this Section we will cover some of the other areas considered as worship. This Section may challenge your thinking and prior experiences of church meetings and indeed may raise some questions about what others are doing during the 'worship time' of meetings. So, I will take a moment to remind you of your mission to express God's love. Do not use this information to put yourself on a pedestal of knowledge so that you can look down at others. We aim to love people, to help people and to pray for them. Now let's start by considering:

God is waiting for us: This is a beautiful thought. Sometimes we think of God as being a faraway person with a white beard somewhere out in the middle of the Universe and that He is not concerned with us. However, God is deeply concerned with our lives. King David realised this after the defeat of his enemies when he said, *"Who am I, O Lord GOD, and what is my house, that you have brought me thus far?"* **2 Samuel 7:18** ESV. The truth is that God loved us so much that He sent his son Jesus to die for us, and now because of that sacrifice, we can enter the holy place, into the very presence of God the Father. God is waiting for us, just as He told John: *"Behold, I stand at the door, and knock: if any man hear my voice, and open the door, I will come in to him, and will sup with him, and he with me"* **Revelation 3:20** KJV.

We must actively seek God: As we have seen in the verse above from Revelation, God is waiting for us, but we must open the door! So many people just sing songs, following a musician who is leading worship. Quite often in those situations, we are not actively seeking God, but instead, we are following the projected words on the screen. Jeremiah prophesied, *"You will seek me and find me, when you seek me with all your heart"* **Jeremiah 29:13** ESV. Imagine people breaking out of their worship routines and declaring 'I am not leaving here until I meet with You Jesus and hear what You have to say to me'. That is what I would love to see. Instead, we often find people obeying a structure which is predetermined and not necessarily by God. When we look at examples of fellowships from the early church, we can see that it was more inclusive than exclusive. What does that mean? Well, imagine a meeting where everyone is taking part, all equal and in submission as God leads. Paul wrote to the Colossians, saying *"Let the word of Christ dwell in you richly in all wisdom; teaching and admonishing one another in psalms and hymns and spiritual songs, singing with grace in your hearts to the Lord"* **Colossians 3:16** KJV.

Knowledge Challenge #4

Open your Bible and write out these verses: **John 4:23-24**

_____
_____
_____
_____
_____
_____

Now, using your own experiences, try to list three ways in which you believe people can worship in Spirit:

For example: speaking in tongues

1._____

2._____

3._____

Secondly, make a list of three things which worshipping in Spirit does not include:

For example: using human thinking to pick themed songs for a meeting

1._____

2._____

3._____

Now, write three things that you feel worshipping in truth must include:

For example: singing a spontaneous song from your heart

1._____

2._____

3._____

Now, write three things which display dishonesty in worship:

For example: dishonest lyrics like 'I bow down on my knees' but people are remaining standing

1._____

2._____

3._____

Imagine a wife called Jennifer, who thinks that she is the most loving wife in the world. Once a week, Jennifer takes her husband out to watch romantic movies in the cinema. Now Jennifer has a wonderful memory and would often remember sayings from the movies. After many years, she began to use the words from the movies to express her love to her husband. The words sounded very romantic, but when he realised what she was doing he didn't feel very loved at all. She hadn't used her own words to express her love to him in years.

If we don't use other people's words to express love in our closest relationships, why should we then use other people's words to show our love to God? If you are singing a song in a meeting and you aren't feeling those things, then you are just lying to God in His house and to His face! God can see our motives and what is happening in our hearts. He knows when we are trying to come into His presence with unresolved issues such as unforgiveness and sin.

Modern churches often measure 'worship' by these things:

- The quality of the performance by the musicians. For example, did the guitarist play all the right chords at the right time?
- How well the music equipment worked, including the projected lyrics and whether the microphones gave feedback during singing.
- The congregation measure it by the little tingle they might feel at the height of emotion brought on by the music.
- The pastor might measure it by the number of people who get involved with clapping and raising their hands.
- The musician might measure it by how emotional the congregation get.

Indeed, the church leadership and congregation often discuss 'worship' after meetings. Over the years I have heard many comments, such as:
- The worship leader was great this morning.
- I didn't like what that singer wore.
- What happened to the smoke machine?

- I don't admire that new song.
- I don't like that old song!
- Did you see that lady who fell over?
- Where did the sound desk guy go?
- Who forgot to buy the microphone batteries?

Many of us get distracted with such unimportant things and to move past all of them we need to understand how God measures worship – after all, worship is for God, so His opinion is what counts.

Go to **Revelation 11:1** and write out the verse below:

_____
_____
_____
_____

Based upon this verse, what are the three things that God measures?

1._____

2._____

3._____

Extract

I wrote about these three measures a few years in a booklet called 'In Spirit and Truth'. Below is an excerpt from it which explains these three measurements.

It is interesting that both humans and God measure worship, albeit with different criteria. In the verse below, we see how God's way of measuring worship includes evaluating the importance, effect, and value of the temple of God, the altar, and the worshippers.

"Then I was given a measuring rod like a staff, and I was told, "Rise and measure the temple of God and the altar and those who worship there" Revelation 11:1 ESV.

The Temple, of course, used to be a physical building in Israel. Today, as we know, the Holy Spirit fills us, and we become the temple of God (1 Corinthians 6:19-20). Both the old temple (building) and the new temple are associated with holiness (1 Corinthians 3:16-17). The ultimate holiness existed in the inner courts of the temple (building) just as today the holiest part of us is the reborn spirit that resides in us. This holiness should be reflected throughout our hearts, minds, actions, thoughts and words (1 Peter 1:14-16). Paul wrote to the Ephesians saying, *"Strive for peace with everyone, and for the holiness without which no one will see the Lord"* Hebrews 12:14 ESV. These changes are part of an ongoing process of sanctification which helps us to draw closer to the Lord and to go deeper in our worship.

The verse from Revelation 11 urges us to measure the value of the temple, which now refers to the hearts of believers. So, what value do we place on the temple?

We know that when we assign a high value to something, we treat it with respect and protection. For example, telling the children to take their shoes off to keep the new carpet clean, or not letting others drive our brand new car. So let me ask again, what value do we place on the temple (meaning our bodies, minds and hearts)? Do we treat our physical body with respect and with care? It is the temple of the Lord God Almighty. Do we take steps to protect our mind from things that would corrupt it? It is the temple of the Lord God Almighty. Do we treat our heart with care and protection? It is the temple of the Lord God Almighty.

We should treat the temple with care and respect, and we should ensure that our hearts are inclined to God. One way of doing this is through fasting. There are different ways to fast such as (a) fasting physically, (b) fasting mentally, and (c) fasting emotionally. We all know about the physical type of fasting, which is to abstain from food and water. But what about the other two, what are they? Fasting mentally is about declaring 'my mind is a temple' and abstaining from worldly influences which are causing distractions. It could include the TV, computer games, newspapers and books. Finally, fasting emotionally is about adjusting your relationships in a way that displays to God that He is number one in your heart. Obviously, we can't be harsh towards others while fasting as that would not be loving. If two people are dating, they could fast from each other for a few days. Then for married couples, they could for example, fast from each other for a few hours on a Saturday. Obviously both parties would need to be in agreement so that no offence is caused. Lastly, humility should accompany fasting (Matthew 6:16) which means that we should not boast about it on social networks.

So to summarise, in measuring the value of the temple, we should continue to move into holiness allowing God to strip away from us what He must. We must treat our bodies, hearts and minds with love care and respect. We must be active in fasting to show God that He is number one in the temple.

The Altar in the Old Testament was a place where a person would make a blood sacrifice to God.

For example, Moses instructed Aaron *"Draw near to the altar and offer your sin offering and your burnt offering and make atonement for yourself and for the people, and bring the offering of the people and make atonement for them, as the LORD has commanded"* Leviticus 9:7 ESV.

The purpose was to give an offering for our sins. Perhaps we can understand this through the Passover. The angel of death passed by the doors marked with blood (from innocent lambs) in Egypt. This sacrifice was of course representative of the blood that Jesus would eventually shed for us, after which the old style altar was no longer needed (Hebrews 10:10-15). Many Christians today associate the altar with being the communion table. Others perhaps see it as a place, the stage at the front of the room where people sometimes kneel to repent of their sin. However, the altar is actually in our hearts.

There was a problem with the altar in the temple of the Old Testament. The people would come and bring their sacrifices, but then they would go home and continue to sin. They thought that it was ok to do so as they could just go and make another sacrifice. God didn't want sacrifices on the altar, He wanted obedience (Hosea 6:6). If we think about it, God required the sacrifice only because of the failure to obey. Jesus was a sacrifice for our sins because of the failure of Adam and Eve to obey in the Garden of Eden (and everyone else since then). Sadly there is a systemic problem with the new altar too. You don't have to look far to see people who have accepted Jesus sacrifice, but then get a false understanding that they can now sin to their heart's desire. This false teaching causes feet to rush to evil, and it is an abomination (Proverbs 6:16-19). Jesus said, *"Go and sin no more"* John 8:11 ESV and later went on to teach that *"If you love me, you will keep my commandments"* John 14:15 ESV.

When we have a loving relationship with God, there is a place for fear. Not the type of fear that causes a person to cower under their bed thinking that a wrathful God in heaven will smite them. That kind of fear is contrary to His love for us (1 John 4:18). The healthy type of fear can be thought of as respect. If you love someone, you respect them and will not purposely hurt them. It is through this healthy kind of the fear of God that we can gain wisdom (Psalm 111:110). It promotes an outlook that leads to life (Proverbs 19:23). If you fear God, you won't treat Him as a doormat, or as a ticket to get to heaven.

I also believe that we should make personal sacrifices, not a blood sacrifice, but love offerings. We cannot redeem our sin through sacrifices, but we can show our love to God by laying down parts of our lives. For example, if God asked someone, 'come and spend time with Me.' However, they are in the middle of watching a movie then they will have to make a sacrifice. Of course, the sacrifices be a lot bigger. A missionary called John Lake sold everything he owned when God asked him to go to South Africa. He didn't even keep enough money to pay for the boat tickets for him and his family. Later on, missionaries working for John Lake were willing to lay down their lives in obedience and sacrifice to God. John Lake had to bury many of them. Perhaps these missionaries are among those mentioned at the altar in Revelations:

"When he opened the fifth seal, I saw under the altar the souls of those who had been slain for the word of God and for the witness they had borne. They cried out with a loud voice, "O Sovereign Lord, holy and true, how long before you will judge and avenge our blood on those who dwell on the earth?" Then they were each given a white robe and told to rest a little longer, until the number of their fellow servants and their

brothers should be complete, who were to be killed as they themselves had been" Revelation 6:9-11 ESV.

So to summarise, in measuring the importance of the altar, we must act in obedience and prepare ourselves to sacrifice anything, including being willing to lay down our lives.

The worshippers are obviously us. The verse from Revelation urged us to measure the effect of the worshippers. What does it mean by measuring the 'effect' of the worshippers? The meaning of 'effect' is 'a change which is the consequence of an action'. When applied to worshippers, we should measure the change that happens in them during their time of worship. I remember watching a documentary about the Azusa Street revival. One account mentioned how, during worship, a woman fell to her knees and cried out loudly that God had healed her of blindness. No one had prayed for her. The only thing happening in the room at that moment was worship. Of course, this is not a unique event, but sadly it is not happening enough. Seeing people change during worship is not the norm, nor is it expected by many churches, but it is what God wants. Whether that 'change' is repenting of sin or handing over to God our possessions, each time we enter into the presence of God He wants to change us. So why is it not happening?

Apart from the confines of traditions which we have talked about, there is a certain hardness of heart towards God. If you visited churches, and just observed people, you may notice that many people are not running into God's presence. There is little hunger in their hearts and so they are not willing to forget everyone else in the room. Often people get distracted and look around to see what's happening, or to gawp at latecomers. You will usually find the leaders of the church towards the front, looking dignified, they might clap along with the songs. However, quite often you might notice people approach them to tell them something by whispering in their ear. The focus of the congregation is on the worship team at the front. Children are often sitting on chairs and fiddling. Sound technicians are frequently adjusting knobs on the soundboard, and the list of distractions that you can witness in churches goes on and on. I ask you, where has the depth of worship gone? Where has the desire for what God has to offer gone? Where is the excitement of the bride for the groom?

Often after church services, people discuss the worship and how good it was or talk about the presence of God. I tell you this though, that when a person has genuinely entered into true worship, it changes them. They may have red eyes from crying, or they may not be able to stop smiling or laughing. Do you think that you'll need to ask them if they felt the presence of God?

So to summarise, to measure the effect of worshippers, we must bear witness to people changing during worship. After we cast away traditions, we must actively fight against distractions until we get to the point where we don't care about what other people in the room are doing. To be so hungry for God that we will seek deep levels of worship where He will change us, and through that change, the glory can go back to

Him.

In our task to measure the temple, the altar and the worshippers, we have found that we are falling short of where we should be with our worship of God. We are also falling short with our fellowship meetings. The good news is that God is making these things known so that we can be a generation of change. God is moving, and He has an extraordinary plan, ensuring that we will be able to worship Him in Spirit and Truth.

Jesus said, "But the hour is coming, and is now here, when the true worshipers will worship the Father in spirit and truth, for the Father is seeking such people to worship him. God is spirit, and those who worship him must worship in spirit and truth" John 4:23-24 ESV.

In summary, God measures worship by what is going on in your heart. If we have given a sacrifice (part of ourselves) allowing that part of us to be sanctified, then we have changed during worship. If you haven't changed, then you haven't been worshipping at all – you have just been singing songs. Worship gives God what was due to Him. However, when we truly worship, it can result in benefits for us.

Read about the benefits in **Deuteronomy 11:13-15**, write down your thoughts:

_____

_____

_____

In no way should we ever worship God with selfish motives – such as those who only worship God to feel good about how they have spent their time. Worship in Spirit and Truth is an expression of love. I have said this many times – the songs produced by our modern Christian music Industry are the elevator music on the way up to the Spirit and Truth floor. Worship is a great opportunity for us to express our love to God. However, expressing love is not always pretty, it may include:
- Tears of joy/sadness
- Dancing/jumping/clapping
- Kneeling
- Shouting

Did you know that in some churches that if they see a person with their hands by their side, or in their pockets – they will see it as a form of rebellion against God? Often we are tied to a set space, perhaps to our chair and the space immediately in front of it. Instead, we should find a space where we are comfortable to express our love, whether it be by raising hands or dancing. We must to be able to forget everyone else and everything in the room. Pastors/church leaders need to take their minds off the organisation of the meeting, worship leaders/musicians need to take their mind off what song is next, children need to not think about what their parents will think, and teens should not think about what their friends might think. Worship time is only about God!

Simply put, we get a choice: to just sing along with the planned songs, or we can boldly go to God and seek Him. However, if we truly love God, we should be longing for time with Him. Therefore, we should push aside anything and anyone who stands in our way.

True worship goes beyond mere form and can, therefore, be hindered by a wrong relationship with God, or indeed with others.

Read these verses: **Matthew 15:7-9**, **James 4:3** & **Matthew 5:23-24**. Write down the ways in which your worship to God can be hindered:

_____
_____
_____
_____
_____
_____

Now, turn to our YouTube page and watch **discipleship training, Video 10**

If you go to our YouTube channel 'Revival Well' and then go to our Playlists, you will find one called 'Discipleship Course'. In that Playlist, you will see all the videos relating this course. Click on the one called 'Video10. I have decided. YourValue.' Alternatively, you can view or download the video directly from Google Drive at this link:

https://drive.google.com/open?id=1hUtub8yUfxczn6awBeqm3qSu7w4zICIA

SECTION SIX CHALLENGE

For this challenge, you are going to look for God's treasure. What is God's treasure? People are God's treasure! Here is what you are to do:

Start out by spending three minutes praying. Explain to the Lord in prayer that you would like to find one of His treasures, a person who is in need, and ask Him for clues that will bring you to them. Get a piece of paper, and ask for hints in these categories:
- The name of the person
- The location where you will find them
- What that person will be wearing
- What the person's need is
- Also, watch for any other thing that God might show you and write it down.

Now if you heard a definite location from God, now is your time to go there and find the person. If you did not get a particular location, then go about your day as usual but keep your eye out for a person who matches the rest of the clues. Wait on the Lord and ask Him to guide you. When you find the person, approach them and explain what you're doing, showing them your piece of paper. As a conversation opens, offer to pray with them, or share your sixty-second testimony (speak as the Lord leads you). Write down your experiences in this task and then move on to the next section.

_____
_____
_____
_____
_____
_____
_____
_____
_____
_____
_____
_____
_____
_____
_____

The Power of Words
Section Seven

You have been learning over the past three weeks how to draw closer to God, how to listen to Him, to talk with Him and to worship Him. Now that you have a grasp of intimacy with God, we will now move on to a new Block which covers some essential topics of Christian living. There are some Christians who have learnt about sanctification and to walk intimately with God but have not progressed to understanding how to live in faith, to walk in humility and to control their tongue. There are many elements of Christian living that we could have covered. These next three Sections were chosen because if a believer fails to understand these lessons, then it might hinder them from hearing the call of God.

As your challenge last week, you were set with the task of finding 'hidden treasure'. How do you feel you got on with this? Some of you may have had useful clues and managed to find the person, only to be rejected by them. Others of you may not have found anyone at all. The aim of the lesson, apart from increasing boldness, was to open your mind to what God wants you to do on a daily basis. God has set apart things that only you can accomplish. We should remain humble and always listening for direction, being willing to go and carry out the tasks that He gives us. We should also have the heart to share our testimony with those people who do not know God yet. If you have not done so already, take a few minutes right now in prayer to discuss how your assignment went, submit any mistakes and weaknesses to God for help.

In this week's Section, we are going to look at the power of words. These are (a) the power of the words that we speak and (b) the power of the words that people speak over us. A lot of the time we don't realise the words that we allow into our lives. This Section aims to challenge you as a disciple to examine your own words and those of others. In the Challenge at the end of this Section, you will get an opportunity to measure such words during a full day.

Now, turn to our YouTube page and watch **discipleship training, Video 11**

If you go to our YouTube channel 'Revival Well' and then go to our Playlists, you will find one called 'Discipleship Course'. In that Playlist, you will see all the videos relating this course. Click on the one called 'Video11. I have decided. Anguish.' Alternatively, you can view or download the video directly from Google Drive at this link:

https://drive.google.com/open?id=1hUtub8yUfxczn6awBeqm3qSu7w4zICIA

Once we **understand our value** in being servants of the Living God, it is then that we can stand up to and reject and bind any negative words that people speak over us, or indeed words that we speak over ourselves. It might be saying small things like, 'I woke up on the wrong side of the bed today' or bigger things like 'I never have any luck in finding someone to date, let alone marry'. As children of God, we have access to the full inheritance of God as we have been made fellow heirs with Christ **Romans 8:17**. This family connection is something that king David experienced when he wrote *"I will tell of the decree: The LORD said to me, "You are my Son; today I have begotten you. Ask of me, and I will make the nations your heritage, and the ends of the earth your possession"* **Psalms 2:7-8** ESV.

We should also **evaluate our uniqueness**. The kingdom of the world highlights role models which many try to emulate. On the other hand, the Kingdom of God contains 'peculiar' people created uniquely by God to fulfil a specific role **1 Peter 2:9**. We are not supposed to copy what other people do, nor are we supposed to try and achieve what others achieve. We are supposed to walk a unique path that God has set out for us and to complete the tasks which He has given to us. Many Christians get frustrated trying to be someone else and meanwhile miss their unique calling. You are an original, designed by God, with a unique purpose.

Bearing your value and uniqueness in mind, let's look at how words may impact your life.

Our words can mean life and death

In your Bible, now read **Isaiah 6:5**.

Many Christians would see Isaiah as a great prophet, a man with words that prophesied the future for many nations. However, here in this verse, Isaiah admitted that his tongue was wretched and needed to be cleansed by the hot coal! Most Christians have got into the culture of Christianity and would avoid swearing and so on. Think for a moment though, about how unholy our words can be in comparison to Isaiah, and even more unholy in contrast to God. Indeed, this is perhaps why James wrote *"And the tongue is a fire, a world of unrighteousness. The tongue is set among our members, staining the whole body, setting on fire the entire course of life, and set on fire by hell"* **James 3:6** ESV.

These unholy words that we are speaking over ourselves and others can cause either life or death, did you know that? Let's have a look at some scriptures to help our understanding:

Write out this verse: **Proverbs 18:21**

_____
_____
_____

Write out this verse: **Proverbs 13:3**

_____
_____
_____

Write out this verse: **Proverbs 21:23**

_____
_____
_____

Write out this verse: **Proverbs 15:4**

_____
_____
_____

Our words can be harsh and unloving

One time when I was at the library, I sat down at one of the computer desks to do some typing. There was a lot of other people there, also working on computers. To my right, there was a teenager, and he was playing a game on his phone which was making lots of noise. I must admit that I was slightly annoyed by the noise and felt like saying something to him, but instead, I kept silent. About ten minutes later, another man who was also sat by the computers stood up and began to speak angrily towards the youth saying, 'Can you turn that off?' The youth ignored him, so the man kept ranting saying, 'You're lucky I became a born-again Christian or else I would come over there and sort you out!'

I think that this was a failure on the man's part to show the love of Jesus. Instead, he displayed anger, not just in front of the teenager but also to a whole room of people. In Proverbs, we are told that *"There is one whose rash words are like sword thrusts"* **Proverbs 12:18a** ESV. We should remember what Paul taught us *"Bless those who persecute you, bless and do not curse them"* **Romans 12:14** ESV.

Write out this verse: **Proverbs 15:1**

_____
_____
_____

Write out this verse: **Proverbs 29:20**

_____
_____
_____

Write out this verse: **Proverbs 17:27**

_____
_____
_____

Our words can be wasteful

Quite often some Christians drift into making judgements about other believers, whether it be a person in their own church who they feel has stepped out of line, or if it's a famous preacher who they feel is a wolf in sheep's clothing. Also, Christians are not immune to gossiping. For example by saying, 'did you hear that the pastor's daughter is pregnant out of wedlock?' or 'I heard the church down the road has had money problems and is closing its doors this month'. I think that we need to love the body of Christ, meaning that every believer who is a part of the body is a part of us, and so we should love them just as we love ourselves **1 John 3:16**. The Bible sets out clear guidelines for a wayward believer, but instead of following those guidelines, many talk spitefully and gossip about them. Never mind what they are doing wrong, look at the words coming that are out your own mouth!

When writing to the Ephesians, Paul stated this *"Let no corrupting talk come out of your mouths, but only such as is for building up, as fits the occasion, that it may give grace to those who hear"* **Ephesians 4:29** ESV. If we are busy tearing down other believers, we are not allowing them the grace to which God has freely given all of us. Shall they be judged and not you?

Write out this verse: **Colossians 3:8**

_____
_____
_____

Write out this verse: **Proverbs 17:9**

_____
_____
_____

Write out this verse: **Ephesians 5:3-4**

_____
_____
_____
_____
_____

Thoughts become words and then can become reality

We should realise that the words that we speak over ourselves can come true. There is a bit of a mystery about this. Perhaps it might be because we have the ability as believers to prophesy. Perhaps it is because we allow those words to convince us and guide our paths. For example, a teenager who declares 'I am going to be a doctor'. Years later after school and college, he becomes a doctor. Every word we speak comes from a thought so we should examine where it originated. We already looked at discernment between God's voice, our voice and the voice of the devil. If we allow a thought from the devil to become a word, then we might follow that word onto an ungodly path.

Sometimes it's not just what we say, but how we say it that matters. For example, if we continuously speak over ourselves 'I need to lose weight', you will fulfil those words, and you will always need to lose weight. Instead, we should say 'I am losing weight'. It seems like a small difference, but when we fulfil our own words, the way we speak our words becomes so important. Let's have a look at some common expressions that we should perhaps re-consider:

- I am dying to use the bathroom, instead, say 'I am going to use the bathroom.'
- I need to lose weight, instead, say 'I am losing weight.'
- I need a coffee/cigarette/drink (in the way an addict says it), instead, say 'I am feeling cravings, but Jesus is sufficient for all my needs.'
- I got up on the wrong side of the bed, instead, say 'I had a bad start to the day, but Jesus is going to change that.'
- I am not feeling well, instead, say 'I have not felt good today but Jesus, You are my healer and I cry out to You and humbly ask for healing.'
- I never have any luck, instead, say 'I don't need any luck because I have the favour of God.'
- I hate Mondays, instead, say 'every day is a blessing and has a purpose, Lord Jesus show me my purpose today.'
- I never have enough_____, instead, believe and rest in God's promise of meeting all our needs.
- I want_____, instead, say 'The Lord is my shepherd; I shall not be in want' **Psalm 23:1** ESV.
- I am no good at _____, instead, put your trust in God and ask the Holy Spirit to empower you. He will make your life significant.

It is amazing how powerful the word 'but' is. You can take any negative sentence you are saying, stick in the 'but' and then add how God can change it. Did you know that God records every word we speak and we will have to answer for them? Jesus said, *"I tell you, on the day of judgement people will give account for every careless word they speak. For by your words you will be justified, and by your words you will be condemned"*

Matthew 12:36-37 ESV. We cannot hope to control our tongue by our own strength, which is why James wrote *"But no human being can tame the tongue. It is a restless evil, full of deadly poison"* **James 3:8** ESV.

Our hope is through Jesus. Jesus is the master of words because He is the Word that was there from the beginning **John1:1**. When we choose to follow Jesus, some amazing things started to happen. Jesus speaks words to us that go into our hearts and our mouths **Romans 10:8** which begin to replace the old words that we used to speak. His words pierce deep into our hearts changing us forever **Hebrews 4:12** and if we follow His words we are surely His disciples **John 8:31**. His words become life to us **John 6:63** so we focus more and more on His words instead of our fleshly desires **Matthew 4:4**. Then as we hear His sweet words, our faith grows **Romans 10:17** and He lights the path as we walk forward **Psalm 119:105**.

So, what words should we be speaking and what importance do those words have in our lives?

- Words should produce good fruit: **Proverbs 25:11, Luke 6:45, Matthew 12:34 & Proverbs 18:20**
- Words should bring healing: **Proverbs 12:18b, Proverbs 12:25 & Proverbs 16:24**
- We should conquer by our words: **Isaiah 54:17 & 1 Corinthians 4:20**

Pick four of the above verses, look them up and write down how you think words can be used in a positive way:

_____
_____
_____
_____
_____
_____

I think that one of the most important verses listed above is this one, *"you shall confute every tongue that rises against you in judgement"* **Isaiah 54:17b** ESV. This verse means that we have the right to, and should always stand up against any words spoken over us that are contrary to the plan and promises that we know God has for our lives. We can bind those words with the power of Jesus, and what is bound on earth is also bound in heaven. If you visit the dentist and he speaks negative words over your teeth and gums, reject and bind those words from becoming your reality.

SECTION SEVEN CHALLENGE

For one day, actively listen to things that you have spoken over yourself, List any negative things here:

1._____
2._____
3._____
4._____
5._____
6._____
7._____
8._____
9._____
10._____

It is important to break any bad habits of how you speak about yourself or even your family. The best way to do this is to ask Jesus to help tame your tongue, and to commit any of those incorrect words to Him, and ask Him to help you stop speaking them!

For one day, actively listen out to negative things that other people have spoken over you, List them here:

1._____
2._____
3._____
4._____
5._____
6._____
7._____
8._____
9._____
10._____

It is important to tackle any negative things spoken over us as soon as possible, and this can be done in prayer, it can even be as simple as praying "I reject those words in the name of Jesus", do that now with any of the things you have listed above.

How does God see you? What values do you think God sees in you? List five of these values.

1._____
2._____
3._____
4._____
5._____

It is vital for us to understand our value in Christ, to find out who we are in Christ because it will help us break any negative thoughts or words that we might think/say about ourselves.

Read the verses listed and complete the sentences:

Luke 12:6-7
God knows how many _____ I have on my _____

Psalm 139:13-14
God made me in_____, I am _____ and _____ made

Matthew 7:7
If I _____ for something then _____

John 16:33
God has _____ the world so that I may have _____

Jeremiah 31:3
God has loved me with an _____

Zephaniah 3:17
He will _____ me, he _____ over me, because He loves me

John 3:16
He loves _____ so much that he sent _____ to _____ for _____

Ephesians 1:5-6
_____ chose _____ to be His _____ son/daughter

If you are experiencing low self-esteem, or have done so in the past, you could choose a few Bible verses which counteract the negative thoughts you have about yourself. Every day you can read those verses and declare them over yourself. They are God's promises, and He is faithful.

Humility
Section Eight

As your challenge last week, you were set asked to identify words being spoken over you. How did this go? Were you surprised at some of the things people said? You were also set a challenge to consider *your* value in God's eyes. From this, I hope that as you move forward in your walk, that you will reject any word contrary to God's plan for you, and God's promises for you. Bear in mind, that this does not mean that we can reject a person who has come to rebuke or correct us because we should have a teachable heart. Furthermore, we should not rebuke people's words in an unloving way, but instead be wise about how we do so.

Indeed, many people in ministry have not kept a teachable heart and have allowed pride to sneak in the door. If you travel around visiting churches, you might notice a lack of humility as a common struggle for Christians. As part of your discipleship course, we want to ensure that we cover this important topic. The last thing we need is more people acting in ministerial roles with hearts full of pride.

When Samuel was sent by God to appoint a new king of Israel, Samuel had to find a humble man, and he observed it in Saul: *"And Saul answered and said, Am not I a Benjamite, of the smallest of the tribes of Israel? and my family the least of all the families of the tribe of Benjamin? wherefore then speakest thou so to me? And Samuel took Saul and his servant, and brought them into the parlour, and made them sit in the chiefest place among them that were bidden, which were about thirty persons"* **1 Samuel 9:21-22** KJV.

Recently a friend of mine bought a car and boasted about it to all his friends, within a week, the car had broken down, and he was left to admit that his car wasn't so great after all. We all must learn this lesson in life, and it is a fulfilment of God's laws that He built into the Universe, *"When pride comes, then comes disgrace but with the humble is wisdom"* **Proverbs 11:2** ESV. Naturally, we all gravitate towards wanting fame and recognition. However, this gravitation is not godly, nor is it of the Kingdom of God. I have come across many people who parade what they have done for God and boast in the ministries that they have started. I fell into the same trap too, especially in my youth when I didn't know any better.

Be wary of ever doing such things! Instead, recognise that God will lift you up if you walk a humble life with Him **Psalm 147:6**. If you remain humble, God will teach you His Ways **Psalm 25:9**. If a person has pride in their hearts, then God opposes them. Furthermore, grace is only available to those walking in humility **James 4:6b**. This is because God will only dwell in a humble heart **Isaiah 57:15**. So many Christians have made the error of doing ministry, but in their heart, they are doing it to boast or to have pride in their achievements. This is not God's plan for us. We are to aim no higher than a servant of Jesus. There is not meant to be any greatness in our works. There is just supposed to be obedience. One day you could be scrubbing the toilets in your church, the next you could be preaching to 5000 people.

When we walk a humble life with God, there are three aspects to that humility. Let's now have a look at these in more detail.

Humble Behaviour

Look up the following verses in your Bible and make notes on how a humble person should behave:

Philippians 2:3-11 & Romans 12:3

_____
_____
_____

Luke 14:10-11

_____
_____
_____

1 Peter 5:5 & Romans 11:18

_____
_____
_____

1 Peter 3:8

_____
_____
_____

Romans 12:10

_____
_____
_____

Mark 10:43 & Matthew 20:27

_____
_____
_____

Humble Living

Think about Paul who walked in strength and humility. In the world's view, a humble person is often envisaged as a weak person. However, walking with humility in every aspect of your life will you an ambassador of Christ. Can you think of anything that is a foundation that builds others up, but is very strong? The obvious example is a rock. You can build upon a rock because it is strong, and this image of a rock perfectly symbolises what a humble life is like – to build others up, to walk through life allowing God's strength to be your strength. Living like this means you won't push others to one side, just to get ahead of them in ministry or in your workplace. Instead, you allow them to go ahead of you with joy in your heart. Many people would consider Paul as one of the greatest of the apostles, but with his own words Paul admitted that because of his history of persecuting Christians he was the least of the apostles **1 Corinthians 15:9**. Look up the following verses in your Bible and make notes on how a humble person should live their life:

Proverbs 22:4

_____
_____
_____

1 Peter 5:3&6

_____
_____
_____

James 4:10

_____
_____
_____

Luke 1:52

_____
_____
_____

Jeremiah 45:5

_____
_____
_____

Job 40:4

_____
_____
_____

1 Thessalonians 4:11

_____
_____
_____

Humble Words

Think back to the last Section and the importance of the words that we speak. In terms of humility, we should speak humbly in every situation, never boasting in good deeds or in people. The only person our lips should boast about is Jesus Christ. Yes, that means no boasting in the footballer who scored the winning goal, or the good-looking man/woman who you went on a date with. Look up the following verses in your Bible and make notes on how a humble person should speak:

2 Chronicles 7:14 & 34:27

_____
_____
_____

1 Corinthians 13:4

_____
_____
_____

Galatians 5:26

_____
_____
_____

We should take the issue of boasting amongst believers very seriously. The Bible makes it clear that no human being should boast while in the presence of God **1 Corinthians 1:29**. We are told not to boast in our own wisdom, strength or riches **Jeremiah 9:23**. We are also told not to praise our own actions with our mouths **Proverbs 27:2**. So what are we allowed to boast in? We can boast in Jesus **Galatians 6:14**. We are also told that we can boast in our weaknesses **2 Corinthians 12:5-12 & 11:30**. Indeed, we should preach from a foundation of our own weakness, and not from a basis of our own strength. Therefore acknowledging God's strength in us, for His Glory.

Most people hide their weaknesses, why on earth would we want to boast in them? Remember the process of sanctification that we discussed. If we are admitting our flaws as the Holy Spirit convicts us, then we allow God to change our weaknesses into strengths. By boasting in your weaknesses, you will most likely include how God gave you strength to overcome them, thereby glorifying God in the process.

To explain humility in a real-life situation, let's imagine a man called Jim who has joined your church as a new believer. Jim has accepted Jesus as his Lord and Saviour – giving up his life so that Christ lives in him. Jim flourishes in the church and learns how to play the guitar. Within two years he becomes the most skilled Christian guitarist in the world. Now imagine you are Jim's pastor. What words of encouragement might you say to him? Write down your answer:

_____
_____
_____

Now, instead of being his pastor, imagine you are from a church in a neighbouring city. You have heard about Jim's guitar skills and drive to his city to hear him play. You attend the service and then go up to speak to him afterwards, what might you say to him? Write down your answer:

_____
_____
_____

You may have said things like:
- Wow you are so good at playing the guitar.
- Your music is so beautiful.
- When I learn guitar, I want to play like you.
- I can't wait for you to make an album. I will buy loads of copies and give them out to my friends.
- I am glad you are in my church because you draw a crowd.

Let's expand the scenario, imagine that Jim is approached by a Christian music producer who offers to record his music and release an album. Jim is excited by the offer. It might open doors to a full-time ministry. Jim makes his album, and it is an instant hit. Crowds now flock to buy his music and to attend his concerts. He gets so popular that his pastor asks him to cease assisting the worship team on a Sunday morning because the crowds were too big for the church to handle. Jim takes his music to the road, travelling from city to city playing music.

I hope by now that you are recognising the error in this example? If you are not seeing the error, quickly scan over your notes above on how a humble person should live, speak and act. Now, in your opinion, what is wrong with Jim's situation in terms of humility?

_____

_____

_____

The root of the problem can be highlighted by these two verses:

"Not that we are sufficient in ourselves to claim anything as coming from us, but our sufficiency is from God" **2 Corinthians 3:5** ESV.

"I have been crucified with Christ and I no longer live, but Christ lives in me" **Galatians 2:20a** ESV.

Jim gave up his own life when he accepted Jesus as his Saviour. Jim was crucified with Christ and no longer lives. For Jim to claim that he lives, would be to deny his salvation. For others to say that Jim lives, they are taking something that Jesus is doing and assigning glory elsewhere. Jim is not the best guitarist ever, rather Jesus who now lives in Jim is the best guitarist ever. Jim no longer lives, Christ does. The music is therefore only meant to give glory to God. If it goes anywhere else, then it becomes idolatry!

Think back to the time of Moses. God saved the Israelites from the Pharoah, but then afterwards they made a golden calf and attributed the great miracles carried out in Egypt to the works of the golden calf **Exodus 32:4**. They certainly got into trouble for that! In our example, if we attribute what is achieved by Christ incorrectly to Jim, then we are making him into a golden calf and committing idolatry.

With this, you could put a question mark against most of the Christian Production Industry – be it books or music or art. We are justified to question if it is idolatry or not. However, we should take care not to judge others in this matter. Therefore, guard your hearts. Do not set another believer above Christ. Do not go to a worship event just to hear a singer or a band. If you are going, go there to spend time with Jesus. Do not approach other believers and tell them how great they are, instead tell them how great God is for what He is doing in their lives. Do not boast on social networks about your church, or your leaders, or in Christian music. Instead, boast of your weaknesses and boast in Jesus. Do not set out to video yourself helping the poor, or to post your singing online for the approval of others. Instead, let your works be done in secret as much as you can so that you build up a treasure in heaven and not on earth. Do not judge the 'Jim's' of the Christian industry for they might be acting in innocence despite the idolatry gathering around them.

Take a few minutes now in prayer concerning your own life. Identify any areas of your life where you might have taken part in pride or idolatry and repent to God. The list below may help you think through various possibilities:

- Boasting of family achievements
- Boasting in sports/sport stars
- Boasting of academic achievements
- Boasting about church events
- Boasting about your ministry
- Boasting about a teacher/pastor
- Boasting about ourselves and what we have achieved
- Boasting about artistic masterpieces / architecture / music
- Boasting about our possessions
- Boasting about our relationships
- Boasting about our children

Now, turn to our YouTube page and watch **discipleship training, Video 12**

If you go to our YouTube channel 'Revival Well' and then go to our Playlists, you will find one called 'Discipleship Course'. In that Playlist, you will see all the videos relating this course. Click on the one called 'Video12. I have decided. Confidence.' Alternatively, you can view or download the video directly from Google Drive at this link:

https://drive.google.com/open?id=1hUtub8yUfxczn6awBeqm3qSu7w4zICIA

SECTION EIGHT CHALLENGE

It's time to start thinking and praying about your own personal calling. Set aside a time to spend with God – a full day would be preferable. At the start of the day pray and ask God where you should go, what you are to do and what you are to pray about, then follow His instructions or what you feel on your heart to do. During this time, remind yourself of each of the practical challenges you have had to do so far on this course. If necessary, look back at the notes you made at the time. Think about any weaknesses that came up in those challenges, such as lack of time, lack of motivation, lack of boldness or any other difficulties you faced. Admit these weaknesses before God and ask Him to replace your weaknesses with His strength. Ask God to set you free from all the things that have been holding you back so that you can really move forward into your calling with Him. Ask God about His plans for your life, and spend time listening and waiting on Him. Please note down anything you feel is changing within you and anything which you feel God is calling you towards:

Faith
Section Nine

As your challenge last week, you were set with the task of taking a full day to spend with God in prayer, and to seek Him about your calling. How do you feel you got on with this? It is important that we continually ask God to guide our steps, and indeed to correct our actions where required. In humility walk before Him in obedience.

In this week's Section, we will be discussing faith. I find that faith is a difficult word to describe. I know that I have faith in God, but I also know that I must live in faith, and speak words of faith. An atheist looking at my beliefs might challenge me and say that 'faith is just a hope that something is out there.' However, faith is so much more than just a hope. Faith is a confidence whereas hope is a much less secure foothold. For example, 'I hope the plumber comes soon', in comparison to 'I have faith that the plumber will be here in a few minutes.' Here we see it acting as a statement of confidence. Of course, we have that confidence because of the faithfulness of God who always fulfils His words and always fulfils His promises ensuring that *"For whosoever shall call upon the name of the Lord shall be saved"* **Romans 10:13** KJV.

Now faith can be officially defined[8] as:
- Complete trust or confidence in someone or something.
- A strong belief in the doctrines of a religion, based on spiritual conviction rather than proof.

Immediately, we can tell that this definition is not written by a believer. All believers

---

[8] Online definitions https://www.google.ie/?gws_rd=ssl#q=definition+faith Accessed July 2016

should have their personal confidence in Jesus. Faith does not originate from evidence, but having faith and experiencing God will open your eyes to evidence.

Let me give you an example. One night you have a dream, and Jesus tells you to visit a man named John who works at your local supermarket. You wake up and write this down, and pray and ask God for guidance. Then God gives you a vision that John will be wearing a red jumper. You note this down too. You open your Bible for confirmation, and you see the verse "seek and ye shall find". So, the next day you go to the supermarket, and there you find a man named John wearing a red jumper. In this situation, you didn't have faith because you located him as instructed, you had faith beforehand and believed that he would be there. However, the experience of trusting in God and seeing His faithfulness becomes your confidence and evidence.

What we must realise is that the more we talk with God and allow Him to guide us, the more confidence, indeed the more faith we will have in Him. If you had the experience as above, you would not doubt similar guidance the second time around. Our faith grows over time, but only through experiencing God in our daily lives. If we aren't experiencing God, then we are not growing in our faith and leave ourselves open to falling away.

Many young adults have grown up having experienced church, but once they take one step out into the world they hear a voice saying, 'God is not real'. Then they think to themselves, 'well I never did experience God at all, and I was at church every week for twenty years'. However, if an atheist says to a believer 'God is not real', and that believer is walking in faith and experiencing God daily, do you think they would even consider those words? No of course not. In fact, they might say in response, 'that's strange you think that because God was talking to me last night and He told me that I would meet you today and that you need to stop hating God just because your mum died when you were seven-years-old'. That is an example of supernatural strength based on a growing faith in Christ Jesus.

"Now faith is the <u>assurance</u> of things hoped for, the <u>conviction</u> of things not seen" **Hebrews 11:1** ESV. Think of a situation where you have gotten ill. In such an event, we must do more than hope. We must face the situation with faith. Many people get antibiotics from a doctor if they have an infection. They take the tablets and feel a surety inside themselves that everything will start to get better within twenty-four hours. In a similar way that people trust medicines and doctors, we need to learn how to trust God that we will get well. We need to believe in God to do a miracle. We need to trust God for supernatural provision. We need to live as though we have a sure foundation, knowing that God is faithful to us in everything.

This belief means removing our trust in doctors and other professionals and instead depending on God. Does this signify that we never use a doctor again? No, but it does mean that our first stop with all our needs is God. God might send you to the doctor! I remember once getting an infection in my gum which had become swollen and quite sore. My friend prayed with me and the pain left, but the inflammation remained. I went to the doctor, and he looked at my mouth and said, 'Wow that must be sore?' and I responded, 'It was until my friend prayed for me, then Jesus took away my pain'. Perhaps I only got the infection so that (a) I could grow in faith and (b) that the doctor could hear about Jesus taking away my pain.

Does God heal in every situation? The simple answer is no. Our hope is not that these fleshly bodies will last forever. Our hope is in the resurrection. It is important in all difficult situations to submit to God and seek His will. Sometimes we may be healed immediately. Other times it might take time. Other times we may not be healed. In every circumstance, we must submit to the perfect will of our Father. If we do suffer from an illness which persists, His promises declare that He will never leave us nor forsake us. Indeed, He will be our comfort and give us joy even in the most difficult of situations.

Doubt

Unfortunately, it is during challenging situations that many people have fallen into doubt. 'Doubt' is defined as *a feeling of uncertainty or fear*. We all trip up sometimes and can fall into doubt. However, the point is that when this happens to us, that we should turn to God and ask Him to teach us how to display our faith through tough situations. Just as James taught: *"If any of you lacks wisdom, let him ask God, who gives generously to all without reproach, and it will be given him. But let him ask in faith, with no doubting, for the one who doubts is like a wave of the sea that is driven and tossed by the wind. For that person must not suppose that he will receive anything from the Lord, he is a double-minded man, unstable in all his ways"* **James 1:5-8** ESV.

Think back to an event in your own life where you faced difficult circumstances – do you feel you walked in faith during that season? Or did you fall into doubt? Write your thoughts here:

_____
_____
_____
_____
_____
_____

Now, turn to our YouTube page and watch **discipleship training, Video 13**

If you go to our YouTube channel 'Revival Well' and then go to our Playlists, you will find one called 'Discipleship Course'. In that Playlist, you will see all the videos relating this course. Click on the one called 'Video13. I have decided. Faith.' Alternatively, you can view or download the video directly from Google Drive at this link:

https://drive.google.com/open?id=1hUtub8yUfxczn6awBeqm3qSu7w4zlClA

So far, we have looked at how we can be confident in God, showing our faith in all circumstances by standing upon the personal experiences with God, indeed, *"faith comes from hearing, and hearing through the word of Christ"* **Romans 10:17**. Let's move forward now to look at four aspects of faith: (a) the purpose of faith (b) the fruit of faith (c) the building of faith and (d) how to express your faith.

The purpose of Faith

Look up the following verses and write down what the purpose of faith is, or what does faith achieve:

Matthew 21:22 & Mark 11:22-24

_____
_____
_____

Hebrews 11:6

_____
_____
_____

Luke 1:37 & Philippians 4:13 & Mark 9:23 & Luke 18:27

_____
_____
_____

Ephesians 2:8 & John 8:24 & Mark 16:16 & 1 John 5:1

_____
_____
_____

Proverbs 3:5-6 & Psalm 46:10/37:5-6

_____
_____
_____

Romans 4:20-21

_____
_____
_____

These verses show exactly what faith is for: we need faith to please God and when we pray, God will answer us and make all things possible. We need it to build trust, and that trust is not only for our salvation but also for the fulfilment of promises.

The Fruit of Faith

Dormant Christianity does not express faith. There are so many Christians around the world who lay dormant, only attending minimal church meetings and leave no opportunity for their faith to grow. However, when a person is actively walking in faith, it will naturally produce good works. We are saved by faith in Jesus Christ and not works but if our faith is not producing good works, then it has died **James 2:17**.

Fill in the <u>blanks</u> by looking up the verses:

Faith will always produce _____ (**James 2:14-26**) and it will ensure that we _____ (**2 Corinthians 5:7**) with God in a _____ (**1 Timothy 1:19**). Faith creates a _____ (**Psalm 46:1-2**) and makes us heirs to _____ (**Hebrews 11:7**). When we have faith in God we will see many _____ (**Mark 4:38-41**).

Building Faith

Faith is built up by two things, experience and intimacy with Jesus. Think about how Jesus taught the disciples. He sent them out by themselves with little provision, to exercise and experience active faith in God **Luke 10:1-23**. That training step was essential in preparing them for the day when Jesus would be no longer with them. They had to act in faith every step of the way. Churches should give their disciples-in-training a command to go so that they can build up experiences in faith. Sadly, many don't, and that is a failure of churches that must change. During this course, you are being challenged to go out and get experience. When you move on to disciple believers yourself, do not forget to teach this essential step for building faith. Time and time again God will bring us through challenges to develop our faith in His provision and protection, just like He did for the Israelites in the desert.

In Sections Four, Five and Six we covered intimacy in detail. Having those special times with Jesus will also help to build your faith. Love builds up trust and confidence. Think about a newborn baby in the arms of its parents. Over time the child will learn that they can trust their parents through feeling the parent's love for them. In the same way, God loves us, and we must allow His love to fill us so that we can grow in our confidence of Him.

Expressing Faith

Faith can be strengthened through our words and actions. We learnt in Section Seven how important our words are. Based upon that lesson, consider the importance of speaking words of faith rather than words of doubt. Acting in faith is also a beneficial way of expressing faith. I remember when my wife and I were waiting for the purchase of our home to come through. One morning I just hopped in our car, and I went and filled it with petrol in faith, believing that with that petrol we would collect the keys to our new home – and we did! Taste and see that the Lord is good **Psalm 34:8**, express your faith in action and see that God will fulfil what He has promised to you.

However, do not undermine your words or actions by doubt. For example, if I had filled up my car with petrol in faith that day, but returned to my wife and said, 'I don't think we will get our house today', then one would have been cancelled out by the other. If you ever do slip up, just pray and take back your own words and ask the Lord to bind them in heaven and earth. If you are married, each of you can help one another to listen and watch for doubt being expressed through actions or words so that you can point it out to each other. Not to pull each other down, but to help you both grow in faith.

Now, turn to our YouTube page and watch **discipleship training, Video 14**

If you go to our YouTube channel 'Revival Well' and then go to our Playlists, you will find one called 'Discipleship Course'. In that Playlist, you will see all the videos relating this course. Click on the one called 'Video14. I have decided. RunTheRace.' Alternatively, you can view or download the video directly from Google Drive at this link:

https://drive.google.com/open?id=1hUtub8yUfxczn6awBeqm3qSu7w4zICIA

Remember these points from the video, if you seek God will all your heart you will:
- Have control over your life, free from manipulation by the devil.
- Have pure light in you – no darkness.
- Not allow any weapon to prosper against you.

SECTION NINE CHALLENGE

For this week's challenge, we ask that you set aside extra time to spend with God, at least two hours. Perhaps you should return to reflect on the lessons about intimacy with God. You can use this time as you like, but we ask that you use this opportunity to continue to make notes in your journal. Note down anything of importance such as Bible verses which you have read during this time that touched your heart, opportunities you have had with people to share the gospel, dreams which you may have had during the night and so on.

_____
_____
_____
_____
_____
_____
_____
_____
_____

The Life of a Disciple
Section Ten

Welcome to the last Block of this course. The end is now within sight. This week we are going to be looking at the life of a disciple. Some people get muddled up with what a disciples' life looks like – they look to famous preachers and evangelists and imagine their life as being the same one day. As you have hopefully been learning in this course so far, every person is unique and has a unique set of tasks that God has set out for them to achieve – our focus is to listen and obey as best we can.

Now, turn to our YouTube page and watch **discipleship training, Video 15**

If you go to our YouTube channel 'Revival Well' and then go to our Playlists, you will find one called 'Discipleship Course'. In that Playlist, you will see all the videos relating this course. Click on the one called 'Video15. I have decided. God's Promise.' Alternatively, you can view or download the video directly from Google Drive at this link:

https://drive.google.com/open?id=1hUtub8yUfxczn6awBeqm3qSu7w4zlClA

Twelve instructions for Disciples

We are going to look at twelve instructions which Jesus gave to His disciples, and use them as instructions for our own lives. First, we should take note that Jesus still appoints disciples in the same manner as when He walked the earth *"After these things the Lord appointed other seventy also, and sent them two and two before his face into every city and place, whither he himself would come"* **Luke 10:1** KJV. What we learn from this is:
1. That Jesus appoints people to their role

2. Jesus sends those people to bring His good news

Although this sounds quite simplistic, you would be surprised at how many Christians go into a role because their church leader appointed it to them. Forty years later, they still hold the same position and continue to live outside of God's plans for their life. Also, many people accept roles where there are no opportunities to share the good news. When we serve God, we should be ambassadors at whatever He asks us to do. If our job is to clean toilets, then we should do it and look for opportunities to share the good news in the process. When the early church needed several disciples to distribute food, they looked for people filled with the Holy Spirit to do the job **Acts 6:3**.

After Jesus had appointed the seventy-two disciples he told them this *"Therefore said he unto them, The harvest truly is great, but the labourers are few: pray ye therefore the Lord of the harvest, that he would send forth labourers into his harvest. Go your ways: behold, I send you forth as lambs among wolves"* **Luke 10:2-3** KJV. What we learn from this is:

3. Very few answer the call of discipleship
4. That Jesus commands us to go
5. That the field is dangerous

Look up this verse in your Bible and write it out below: **Revelation 2:10**

_____
_____
_____
_____
_____

I once read about a pastor in Africa who had been beaten up and robbed by a gang. He miraculously recovered, and found one of the men who had attacked him and forgave him and even asked the police not to press charges. This brought a young man to know Christ. Many people in the Western world have forgotten the price that it can cost to be a disciple of Jesus. It is this same cost which holds back so many believers from obeying God's commandment to go. They think of everything they might lose. If I said to you today, 'tomorrow I want you to sell everything you have and go to the airport. At the airport, I will send a man to meet you and he will buy you a one-way ticket to Venezuela.' Would you go? Would you sell everything? Would you even hand in your notice at work? Being a disciple means a willingness in your heart to obey – no matter what it costs – even if it costs your life to lay a foundation for one more person to know Christ – then so be it! Are you ready to pay the cost?

Write your initial thoughts here:

_____
_____
_____
_____

After Jesus told them to go, He gave them specific instructions about provisions: *"Carry neither purse, nor scrip, nor shoes: and salute no man by the way. And into whatsoever house ye enter, first say, Peace be to this house. And if the son of peace be there, your peace shall rest upon it: if not, it shall turn to you again. And in the same house remain, eating and drinking such things as they give: for the labourer is worthy of his hire. Go not from house to house"* **Luke 10:4-7** KJV. Once again, we learn instructions for being a disciple:

6. That there is no need to prepare or to bring provision with you – because provision will come along the way **Luke 12:33-34**
7. That you are to bring the peace of God with you

Now, not bringing your purse or sandals along for your mission is so far removed from today's super-evangelists who travel by private aeroplanes and helicopters, and wear the finest of clothes. So many true missionaries have sold everything they own and have followed God. A good example is John Lake, who sold his wealthy business and gave all the money away. Then went down to the port with his wife and children and waited. A stranger turned up and paid their fares to South Africa. On the other side, another stranger came and paid their immigration fees, and then another stranger was sent by God to collect them and give them a house to live in. There, they began a ministry, and many of their disciples lost their lives – men women and children. However, God used them to spread the good news to people who needed to hear it. Please don't make the error of looking at flashy rich evangelists, but perhaps look to the Christian martyrs as your example of being a disciple.

Now, turn to our YouTube page and watch **discipleship training, Video 16**

If you go to our YouTube channel 'Revival Well' and then go to our Playlists, you will find one called 'Discipleship Course'. In that Playlist, you will see all the videos relating this course. Click on the one called 'Video16. I have decided. Two calls.' Alternatively, you can view or download the video directly from Google Drive at this link:

https://drive.google.com/open?id=1hUtub8yUfxczn6awBeqm3qSu7w4zlClA

A lot of people make a very common mistake. When God gives promises of what their ministry is going to look like, they run after it and try to achieve it with their own strength. To explain this point, consider the example of Abraham, who was promised that he would be the father of many nations. As he grew old he decided to fulfil this promise by his own strength by having a child with his wife's maid **Genesis 16:4**. It did not work out for him. We need to understand that God does things to His schedule and not ours. If we currently stand at location-A and God gives us a promise that we are going to get to location-Z, why do we try and catch the quickest flight to Z without realising there are so many things God wants us to experience and learn along the way? We need to be active yes, but active with waiting on the Lord and following His steps. Secondly, when Abraham received his promised son, he had to be willing to give it all up for the Lord – he was asked to lay down his promised son. Through this obedience and willing heart, God made a greater promise, that of Christ Jesus being born:

> *"And said, I have sworn by Myself, says the Lord, that since you have done this and have not withheld [from Me] or begrudged [giving Me] your son, your only son, In blessing I will bless you and in multiplying I will multiply your descendants like the stars of the heavens and like the sand on the seashore. And your Seed (Heir) will possess the gate of His enemies, and in your Seed [Christ] shall all the nations of the earth be blessed and [by Him] bless themselves, because you have heard and obeyed My voice."* **Genesis 22:16-18** AMP

Have you ever tried in your own strength to fulfil a promise of ministry that God gave you, without clear direction from God? How did this pan out for you? Write down your thoughts:

_____
_____
_____
_____

After Jesus instructed the disciples in what provisions to bring, He also went on to tell them what they are to do in the places they visit: *"And into whatsoever city ye enter, and they receive you, eat such things as are set before you: And heal the sick that are therein, and say unto them, The kingdom of God is come nigh unto you"* **Luke 10:8-9** KJV. This guidance seems straightforward to us, but in the Jewish culture, people would avoid the sick as they were considered unclean. They would also be careful not to eat food that was not prepared correctly. Jesus told them to eat whatever they were given and He told them to go help the sick. There were no cultural considerations made, and this matches up with what Jesus taught in the parable of the Good Samaritan **Luke 10:27-37**. We are being taught to look past our culture and traditions to express the love of God to those who need to hear about Him, so our instructions are:

8. Love the people you meet, no matter who they are
9. Tell them about the Kingdom of God

After this, Jesus explained to them that they would face rejection from people. In doing so, He prepared their hearts for what they would face, telling them: *"The one who hears you hears me, and the one who rejects you rejects me, and the one who rejects me rejects him who sent me"* **Luke 10:16** ESV. I have heard of Christians who have eagerly signed up for an evangelism crusade with their church, only to be spat at or worse. In response, they shrink back – they don't like the rejection or the shame. Indeed, giving up their Saturday just isn't worth it when there are plenty of good movies on TV. Those kinds of reactions come from people who just don't understand that it is impossible for people to reject us – why? Because we no longer live, but Christ lives in us – so they are rejecting the Christ in you, and through that experience we become partakers of the sufferings of Christ Jesus. Instead of being in fear of rejection, we are to love those who reject us! So, our instructions as disciples are:

10. That whenever we face rejection, it is Christ being rejected and not us
11. To love those who hate us **Matthew 5:44**

Now after the disciples had their eleven instructions they went out as Jesus had commanded them. Later they returned to Jesus with eager reports of what they had done saying that even demons had to submit to them in Jesus name. Then Jesus corrected them saying *"Notwithstanding in this rejoice not, that the spirits are subject unto you; but rather rejoice, because your names are written in heaven"* **Luke 10:20** KJV. So many disciples are making the mistake of boasting about what they have done for God on their social networks. Even worse, sometimes they get someone to film them handing out food to the homeless and so on. We can easily get carried away when we see miracles happening as we pray in Jesus name. We feel like boasting 'I prayed and this man walked away from his wheelchair'. If you think this kind of behaviour is valid, then I challenge you to go and read all of the four gospels and show me the part where Jesus boasted about any of the things that He had done. You won't find it. Instead, you will find examples of Jesus asking people not to say anything! Remember you are supposed to remain humble. At the centre of this common mistake is the thought that it is our testimony that this miracle has happened. That is simply not true. If a person is healed, it is their testimony of what God is doing in their lives, and God has simply used your servitude for a moment. Do not forget your place as a humble servant. So, our last instruction is this:

12. To remember that our reward is in heaven and not on earth **Matthew 6:19-21**

Your ministry position, your mission & your priority

So many believers get distracted by going the wrong direction in ministry. Some people work hard to look good at all the meetings hoping that the leadership will notice them. Others push people to one side to claim any spot that becomes available on the worship team. Others wait years for a spot to open in their church only to be overlooked when it does. These issues come from people obeying a religious structure rather than just obeying what God is telling them to do. Others don't even make it to that point of trying. Instead, they spend years trying to perfect themselves because they feel that only perfect people hold ministry positions. Their struggle becomes a never-ending one. There is one thing you should always remember about ministry positions, which is explained very well by *Heidi Baker* who said, 'There is only one direction in ministry: lower still'. Our job is not to climb an outdated and corrupted religious hierarchal structure. Our ministry is giving more and more of ourselves to God and others.

This leads us on nicely to consider what the number one mission of a disciple of Jesus is. Firstly, write out the following verses: **Matthew 25:37-40**

_____
_____
_____
_____
_____
_____
_____
_____
_____
_____

After considering these verses, what is our number one mission?

_____

Hopefully you have guessed correctly, our number one mission is to show love. In terms of our everyday mission to reach unbelievers, we need to love absolutely everyone that comes our way – whether it is at work, or at school, or at college, or even on the street. God has put people in your path that only you can reach.

Imagine a father and daughter who are believers. The daughter goes to school with a hundred children, out of whom she is the only one who believes in God, indeed the only disciple of Jesus who is present. Can her father enter the school to convert the lost? Can you invade the school to convert the lost? The only person who can go to that school and do anything for those hundred children is the daughter. Now apply this to your situations and your circles of influence. Who has God put in your path that only you can reach? Now don't go down the route of shoving the Bible down their necks, or by pointing out their life errors. Our first job is to love them as if they were Jesus.

Disciples should hold tight onto their number one priority (seeking God and loving Him) and their number one mission (to love others). Many Christians have got so caught up with a mission focus that they lose touch with God. All of us have to learn, and some of us the hard way, that if we allow our number one priority to be undermined, then our mission and calling will falter. To ensure that you maintain that good relationship with God, it needs to contain a balance of quality time, intimacy and experiencing God's love. From this foundation, you can share God's love with the people you meet. If you are spiritually starved, how can you possibly hope to feed the people when you have nothing to offer? Jesus is not looking for sacrifice. He is looking for obedience, which in its simplest form is to love God and then to love others.

Write out a plan of how you intend to keep God as your priority:

_____
_____
_____
_____
_____
_____
_____
_____
_____
_____
_____
_____
_____
_____
_____
_____
_____
_____
_____
_____
_____

SECTION TEN CHALLENGE

It is time to start thinking about living as a disciple and reaching those whom God has put in your path to reach. Start by making a list of everyone in your circles of influence – those whom you work with or go to school with, even your neighbours. You can write them here or make a list on a separate piece of paper:

_____
_____
_____
_____
_____
_____
_____
_____
_____
_____
_____
_____
_____
_____
_____
_____
_____
_____
_____
_____
_____
_____
_____
_____
_____
_____
_____
_____

Now begin to pray and ask God to reveal to you His heart for everyone on the list. Ask God to reveal the anguish He feels for the lost. Then be persistent. Keep your list at hand and continue to ask God for breakthrough and for opportunities to love these people with His love, in the hope that they may come to know Christ Jesus, and become a disciple of Him. Wait and watch for opportunities to share your testimony and God's love.

The Call of God
Section Eleven

In this Section, we are going to be looking at the call of God on your life. Most believers want to learn what their calling is supposed to be and then walk in it. Hopefully, by the end of this Section, you will have a clearer idea of *who* God wants to call into service and what He may require of you. Let's begin by looking at the life of Samuel once again.

Now as we know, Samuel was a prophet of God who heard his calling when he was just a boy. However, a time came in his life where God sent him to find the new king of Israel and to anoint him with oil. After finding the least of the least, among the least of the tribes, he anointed Saul to be king. Open your Bible and read what happened to Saul after he parted ways with Samuel: **1 Samuel 10:9-13**.

Knowledge Challenge #5 [Answers on Page 114]

If you were to divide Saul's' experience into four sections, what would they be?

1. (Verse9)
   _____

2. (Verse10)
   _____

3. (Verse11)
   _____

4. (Verse13)
   _____

When I consider these four things regarding my calling, I can certainly identify these four things as marked events that happened to me. We will look at some other scriptural examples of this very same pattern. Before we do, we must understand that before we can experience the call of God, we have to be ready because God is only looking for a certain type of person.

Knowledge Challenge #6

Imagine you are going to be the manager of a 5-a-side football team. The list below indicates the players available to you and their official rating of how good they are. Put a tick next to the five players that you would choose for your team:

Goalkeepers (pick one):
- Smith, rated 2/10
- Kimble, rated 6.5/10
- Jordan, rated 8/10

Defence/midfield (pick two)
- Hughes, rated 4/10
- Adams, rated 1/10
- Harper, rated 7.6/10
- Burton, rated 6/10

Strikers (pick two)
- Ruston, rated 9/10
- Preston, rated 5/10
- Darren, rated 3.7/10
- Ford, rated 7.8/10

Now, you most likely chose the players most of us would: Jordan, Harper, Burton, Ruston and Ford. Many of us might have memories of the schoolyard and two captains picking the players that they wanted for their team. The ones who were not very good at sports were always left to last and perhaps only taken reluctantly, if at all. We can apply this way of picking people to how our modern secular culture operates. If we want legal advice, we will look for the best legal consultant we can afford. If we need an operation, we will want the best medical team that we can get. If we need a builder to fix our home, we will look for the best local builder we can find. If Universities are seeking to attract students, they will want the brightest students attending their programmes. We chose this method because we want to succeed, and to us, we achieve success with the most intelligent and the strongest people on board.

However, this is not how the Kingdom of God operates - thankfully. Here is why: if God were to choose a person because of their strength, then any success will be attributed to that person and not to God. For example, if a football team bring on a striker and he quickly scores two goals, and the team then win the game, the striker will receive most of the glory for his effort. When it comes to great achievements, what is up for grabs is something called glory.

'Glory' is defined[9] as:
- High renown or honour won by notable achievements
- To take great pride or pleasure in

When Apostle Paul wrote to the Corinthians he said, *"Whether therefore ye eat, or drink, or whatsoever ye do, do all to the glory of God"* **1 Corinthians 10:31** KJV. All the honour for what we do is supposed to go to God alone. The avoidance of taking glory for yourself, of course, lines up with what we have been teaching about remaining humble and evading idolatry. What we learn here is that God will only call people that are willing to give Him glory for everything they do. Imagine Moses turning around and claiming that he turned the water red like blood or Samson claiming that it was his strength that allowed him to kill lions or David claiming that his strong arm brought down Goliath.

That's not to say that people who are called by God can't dramatically fail later in life and make a mess of the calling and their lives. Saul certainly made a mess of things, and God replaced him with David. Then, King David made a mess of things by taking another man's wife.

The main point here is to realise that God's criteria is completely different what we might choose. Write down the following verses: **1 Corinthians 1:27-31**

_____
_____
_____
_____
_____
_____
_____
_____
_____
_____
_____
_____

---

[9] Online definitions https://www.google.ie/?gws_rd=ssl#q=definition+glory Accessed July 2016

This is a very hard concept for people to understand because our whole culture is about choosing the strongest and wisest. In many churches, they work to a system of picking the best to be in ministry positions – perhaps that is why so many churches have a focus on achievements and therefore risk falling into idolatry. Perhaps that is the fault of all of us, expecting to attend church and have a man of God teach us a lesson, rather than expecting the least of the people to share what God is saying.

Now, turn to our YouTube page and watch **discipleship training, Video 17**

If you go to our YouTube channel 'Revival Well' and then go to our Playlists, you will find one called 'Discipleship Course'. In that Playlist, you will see all the videos relating this course. Click on the one called 'Video17. I have decided. Tears.' Alternatively, you can view or download the video directly from Google Drive at this link:

https://drive.google.com/open?id=1hUtub8yUfxczn6awBeqm3qSu7w4zICIA

Now, bearing in mind what kind of person God is looking for, let's have a look at examples of the same four steps outlined previously with Saul.

A Weak Man: Peter

We are going to look at the life of Peter as our first example. First turn to **Matthew 26:69-75** in your Bible and read the passage about Peter denying Jesus three times.

What three people accused Peter of knowing Jesus?

_____
_____
_____

In what three ways did Peter deny Jesus?

_____
_____
_____

Have you ever had a moment where you have denied Jesus? For example, hiding your Bible so that people don't see what book you have been reading? Try to think of an example and write it down here:

_____
_____
_____
_____
_____
_____

At the end of this passage of scripture what did Peter do?

_____
_____
_____

Have you ever wondered why Peter didn't just feel remorse, but instead went and 'wept bitterly'? If we had denied Jesus in this way, we may have felt differently but Peter was *with* Jesus when He taught, *"But whoever denies and disowns Me before men, I also will deny and disown him before My Father Who is in heaven"* **Matthew 10:33** AMP. Peter had fallen. He thought that he was strong and would never leave Jesus side, he even cut the ear off a soldier to defend Jesus. But here we see him realising that he was not strong at all, he was weak and couldn't even admit that Jesus was his Lord, his friend and his master. However, Jesus called him as an apostle and had told him directly that *"And I tell you, you are Peter, and on this rock I will build my church, and the gates of hell shall not prevail against it"* Matthew **16:18** ESV. At this point in his life however, Peter's actions and his calling were at odds with each other.

There, with everything laid bare and his weaknesses exposed, God began to change his heart. Later on, he waited and prayed with other disciples, and they were filled with the Holy Spirit on the Day of Pentecost. Then Peter was completely changed, read it for yourself how he had changed: **Acts 3:1-26 & 4:29-31**. Do these steps seem familiar at all – are these not the same steps into walking in your calling that Saul went through?

A Despised Man: Paul

Let's take another quick example just to show you how the examples of Peter and Saul are not alone. Consider for a moment Apostle Paul who said this to the Galatians *"For you have heard of my former life in Judaism, how I persecuted the church of God violently and tried to destroy it"* **Galatians 1:13** ESV. It was at the height of Paul's power when Jesus challenged him, making him blind **Acts 9:3**. There with his spiritual and physical weaknesses exposed, God began to change his heart. Then the Spirit of God filled Him **Acts 13**. Afterwards, he became a completely changed man, going from persecuting the followers of Jesus to being persecuted himself for Jesus' sake.

This very same pattern repeats throughout the Bible. So, we can safely assume that it will be similar for us too.

Now, turn to our YouTube page and watch **discipleship training, Video 18**

If you go to our YouTube channel 'Revival Well' and then go to our Playlists, you will find one called 'Discipleship Course'. In that Playlist, you will see all the videos relating this course. Click on the one called 'Video18. I have decided. Martyrs.' Alternatively, you can view or download the video directly from Google Drive at this link:

https://drive.google.com/open?id=1hUtub8yUfxczn6awBeqm3qSu7w4zICIA

I like to think of the call of God being like the unrolling of a scroll. It is perhaps revealed bit by bit. As we finish one section, a bit more of the scroll is unrolled and we move forward. Can you imagine Apostle Paul being told on his first day 'You are going to Rome in chains where you will die'? That would have perhaps made him run and hide. Instead, Paul was learning the next steps as he went along. We should also consider that when Paul heard the call of God, it did not come from any other human being **Galatians 1:1**, and his immediate response was not even to tell any other human being about it **Galatians 1:16**. How does that differ to modern churches where believers think their pastor will tell them what they will do for the Lord Jesus? How does that differ to ministry leaders who openly boast that they are the founder of their ministry? Write your thoughts here:

_____
_____
_____
_____

At this point I think it would be a good reminder to go back and **watch the first video** of this course which talks about these things:

- God is preparing an army of dedicated people called the remnant who are pure, devoted and fearless.
- There is a judgement on the old system (cold and compromising), but also a new release of a Holy Spirit move.
- It will be a move birthed in prayer.
- If you seek God with all your heart, you're going to feel the pain and grief of God for His church; you'll be misunderstood and accused.
- God looks for people who yearn for Him, for His presence, for His glory, for His move. They are committed, no thought of backsliding, wholly given to God all the days of their lives.

Write your thoughts on this video – how do you feel this applies to your life?

_____
_____
_____
_____
_____
_____
_____
_____
_____
_____
_____
_____
_____
_____
_____
_____
_____

SECTION ELEVEN CHALLENGE

In the challenge last week, you were asked to pray for those who are within your reach - that you could possibly reach out to and love. List down the circles of influence that you currently have right now (for example: workplace, school, college, church, shops):

_____
_____
_____
_____
_____
_____

It is important that we do everything that God enables us to do to reach these people. Since praying and asking God about the people who were on your heart. Has God given you any strategy yet concerning how to reach out to them? If so, note it down here:

_____
_____
_____
_____

If God has not given you a strategy yet, it is important to wait on the Lord, and seek Him until you get instruction. While you wait, continue to pray for everyone in your circles. We cannot run the race until we know what direction to run in. Look up **Psalm 37:34** and write the verse here:

_____
_____
_____
_____

When God does give you a strategy, it is important to remember that your calling is a gradual unrolling, today you may help a lady cross the street, and tomorrow you may preach to 1000 people. One is not greater than the other. There is just the tasks that God gives us, and our obligation is to obey Him. Your plan does not necessarily have to make physical sense, but it does have to make spiritual sense.

Write out these verses:

Proverbs 3:5-6

_____
_____
_____

James 4:17

_____
_____

Luke 18:27

_____
_____

Seven important points regarding starting a ministry

1. Ministry is NOT based on just fulfilling needs alone.

2. Ministry MUST be based on what God wants you to do, what He wants to be fulfilled.

3. Ministry must be founded with LOVE which is stirred up through INTIMACY with God.

4. Whatever you plant in the first instance of ministry, will produce the same sort of fruit. You can't plant an apple tree and expect oranges to grow. If a ministry is planted in the flesh, it will produce the fruit of the flesh. If a ministry is planted by the Spirit of God, and weeds are kept away, then it will produce good spiritual fruit.

5. Ministry and calling changes over time.

6. You only need permission from God to start (remember Paul's story). On the other hand, if you feel that is what God is leading you to link-in with a pre-existing ministry, approach them and see if it would be possible - ensuring that all parties pray together for God's will in the matter.

7. The call of God is for all age groups. There is no ageism in the Kingdom of God.

The Cost
Section Twelve

So, after a lot of studying you have made it to the final week of this discipleship course. By now you should have a good understanding of what it takes to be a disciple. In this Section, we are going to look at the cost of being a disciple. I have often heard people say, 'you need to accept the free gift of salvation from God'. Yes, salvation is free for us to accept. However, it was not free in the sense that Jesus paid a huge price for us. It would be more accurate to say that Jesus came to settle our bill – He has enough credit on His card to pay for everyone. However, there is also a cost for those who choose to be disciples of Jesus. This cost is not for paying for salvation, as Jesus paid that cost, but rather it is a cost to follow Jesus. We are going to look at this in more detail in this Section.

Firstly, let's recap on some important points for you to remember:

Seek the Lord: set your face like flint, be completely determined to seek first the Kingdom of God through maintaining an intimate relationship with God and learning about God through experiences with Him.

Listen to the Lord: when you seek God, He will speak with you. He will guide and instruct you in every step and will tell you if there is anything that you need to change. He will also speak to you about other people so that your heart will be stirred to pray for them and to reach out to them.

Obey the Lord: when you obey the Lord, you are showing that you love Him. After God gives you instruction, it is important to act in obedience to change what needs to be changed and to do everything that He asks you to do. Whenever He has stirred your heart to do something on behalf of His love for other people, it is also important to complete these tasks that He has laid out before you, because he who looks after the small things will be given greater things to do **Luke 16:10**.

Cost: setting your heart on the things above

Look up this passage in your Bible and read it: **Colossians 3:1-7**

Write down the eight things that we are to put to death/no longer do:

1. _____
2. _____
3. _____
4. _____
5. _____
6. _____
7. _____
8. _____

When we turn away from all these things we are giving up the way we used to live. Paul wrote to the Ephesians that they should *"Take no part in the unfruitful works of darkness, but instead expose them"* **Ephesians 5:11** ESV.

Read the next part of the passage **Colossians 3:8-17** and write down the seven things that we are to clothe ourselves with:

1. _____
2. _____
3. _____
4. _____
5. _____
6. _____
7. _____

It is important to remember that God sees our hearts even though other people don't. It is our heart that God will examine. In your Bible look up **1 Samuel 16:7** and see how the Lord corrected Samuel from choosing the wrong king for Israel.

Cost: Taking up your cross:
Knowledge Challenge #7

Find the biggest piece of paper you can and cut out the shape of a cross. Now find a smaller piece of paper and start by writing your name. Then add your job/career, or your school year, or the thing you do with most of your time. Now write down your biggest ambitions in life. Make sure it has enough detail on it that if someone else was to read it that they would recognise it – 'yes that's what he/she does', 'yes that what he/she wants to do'. Now take your little piece of paper with all your details and pin it to the cross that you made.

Letting all those things die and more is what it means for you to take up your cross daily. Paul spoke about this to the Corinthians when he said *"Therefore, if anyone is in Christ, he is a new creation. The old has passed away, behold, the new has come"* **2 Corinthians 5:17** ESV.

In Section Eleven of this course, one of the four elements of taking up your calling was to go through change. It means leaving behind your old life and walking to a high place. For me, God has led me to leave many things behind as I have walked onwards with Him. He will do the same with you and with every disciple. Everything in your life will be shaken until God knows that your heart truly belongs to Him. When this happens, look at what it is that you are holding onto, and open your hands and allow God to change your heart.

Cost: The Promises you *will* Face

When people think of the promises of God, they like to think of all the nice things such as blessings and prosperity. While all of those remain true, there is a set of promises that are for all disciples which help outline the costs you might face in your life. Let's have a look through those now:
- You will be persecuted **2 Timothy 3:12**
- You will be hated **Matthew 10:22**
- You will be insulted **1 Peter 4:12-14**
- You will be slandered **1 Peter 3:16**
- You will suffer for doing good **1 Peter 3:17**
- You will be afflicted in every way **2 Corinthians 4:8-12**
- You will have to forgive your enemies, and feed them and pray for them **Romans 12:17-21**

- You will go hungry and naked and perhaps even be killed **Romans 8:35-37**

In such situations, we are to remain 'more than conquerors'. Jesus told his disciples *"Blessed are you when others revile you and persecute you and utter all kinds of evil against you falsely on my account"* **Matthew 5:11** ESV.

Do not let these things trouble you, for Jesus has gone before us:

"For he grew up before him like a young plant, and like a root out of dry ground; he had no form or majesty that we should look at him, and no beauty that we should desire him. He was despised and rejected by men; a man of sorrows, and acquainted with grief; and as one from whom men hide their faces he was despised, and we esteemed him not. Surely he has borne our griefs and carried our sorrows; yet we esteemed him stricken, smitten by God, and afflicted. But he was wounded for our transgressions; he was crushed for our iniquities; upon him was the chastisement that brought us peace, and with his stripes we are healed" **Isaiah 53:2-5** ESV.

Look up this verse in your Bible and write it below: **Hebrews 12:28**

_____
_____
_____
_____

Jesus clearly advised his disciples about the costs:

If the world hate you, ye know that it hated me before it hated you. If ye were of the world, the world would love his own: but because ye are not of the world, but I have chosen you out of the world, therefore the world hateth you. Remember the word that I said unto you, The servant is not greater than his lord. If they have persecuted me, they will also persecute you; if they have kept my saying, they will keep yours also. But all these things will they do unto you for my name's sake, because they know not him that sent me. If I had not come and spoken unto them, they had not had sin: but now they have no cloke for their sin. He that hateth me hateth my Father also. If I had not done among them the works which none other man did, they had not had sin: but now have they both seen and hated both me and my Father. But this cometh to pass, that the word might be fulfilled that is written in their law, They hated me without a cause" **John 15:18-25** KJV

Again, Jesus spoke to John on the island of Patmos, saying *"Do not fear what you are about to suffer. Behold, the devil is about to throw some of you into prison, that you may be tested, and for ten days you will have tribulation. Be faithful unto death, and I will give you the crown of life"* **Revelation 2:10** ESV. King David also talked about not giving in to fear *"Even though I walk through the valley of the shadow of death, I will fear no evil, for you are with me; your rod and your staff, they comfort me."* **Psalm 23:4** ESV. Apostle Paul advised that when we face the hardest times, when we are in the place of weakness, that's when are strong: *"For the sake of Christ, then, I am content with weaknesses, persecutions, and calamities. For when I am weak, then I am strong"* **2 Corinthians 12:10** ESV.

John had a vision of many people who, in the end times, would not bow down to the beast. He wrote:

> *"Then I saw thrones, and seated on them were those to whom the authority to judge was committed. Also I saw the souls of those who had been beheaded for the testimony of Jesus and for the word of God, and those who had not worshipped the beast or its image and had not received its mark on their foreheads or their hands. They came to life and reigned with Christ for a thousand years"* **Revelation 20:4** ESV.

Now you have been warned of the costs that you may face, *"Go your way; behold, I am sending you out as lambs in the midst of wolves"* **Luke 10:3** ESV.

The End?

Well done! You have reached the end of this course. Hopefully, you have learnt how to walk closer with God. The journey is by no means finished, now is the time to start putting into action all of the things that you have been learning. To seek God with all your heart. To love Him and to love others. To reach people with the good news and to make disciples. As a ministry, we bless you to go forth in the name of Jesus, Amen.

We can provide you with a questionnaire which may help to give you pointers on what areas you are gifted in. It might perhaps serve as a confirmation of what is already in your heart, or perhaps even present you with new ideas. If you would like to complete one, we can send it out to you by email.

If you would like a certificate for completing this course, email us with the following information: First Name, Surname, Nationality, Date of Birth and address. We will then post it to you.

If you feel like you would like to get in touch, we would love to hear from you. Please contact us at:

> Contact email: info@revivalwell.org

Challenge answers

Challenge #1

Answer: 0 1 1 2 3 5 8 13 21 34

Challenge #2

Answer: D

Challenge #5

1. (Verse9) God changed his heart
2. (Verse10) Then the Spirit of God came on him
3. (Verse11) Then he was utterly changed, others were shocked
4. (Verse13) Then he went to a high place (representing a holy walk with God)

Made in the USA
Lexington, KY
31 May 2018